KU-515-964

New Daylight

Edited by Naomi Starkey   September–December 2005

Suggestions for using *New Daylight*

Find a regular time and place, if possible, where you can read and pray undisturbed. Before you begin, take time to be still and perhaps use the BRF prayer. Then read the Bible passage slowly (try reading it aloud if you find it over-familiar), followed by the comment. You can also use *New Daylight* for group study and discussion, if you prefer.

The prayer or point for reflection can be a starting point for your own meditation and prayer. Many people like to keep a journal to record their thoughts about a Bible passage and items for prayer. In *New Daylight* we also note the Sundays and special festivals from the Church calendar, to keep in step with the Christian year.

New Daylight and the Bible

New Daylight contributors use a range of Bible versions, and you will find a list of the versions used in each issue at the back of the notes on page 154. You are welcome to use your own preferred version alongside the passage printed in the notes, and this can be particularly helpful if the Bible text has been abridged.

New Daylight affirms that the whole of the Bible is God's revelation to us, and we should read, reflect on and learn from every part of both Old and New Testaments. Usually the printed comment presents a straight-forward 'thought for the day', but sometimes it may also raise questions rather than simply providing answers, as we wrestle with some of the more difficult passages of Scripture.

Writers in this issue

Peter Graves is Minister of Wesley Methodist Church, Cambridge, and Chaplain to Methodist students at the University. He was formerly Superintendent of the Methodist Central Hall, Westminster.

John Proctor is married to Elaine, with two adult children. He works for the United Reformed Church, teaching the New Testament to students in Cambridge. Before that he was a parish minister in Glasgow. John has written *The People's Bible Commentary: Matthew* (BRF, 2001) and *Urban God* (BRF, 2002).

Veronica Zundel is an Oxford graduate, writer and journalist. She lives with her husband and young son in North London, where they belong to the Mennonite Church.

Rachel Boulding is Deputy Editor of the *Church Times*. For some years she was Senior Editor at SPCK Publishing, commissioning religious books. She lives with her husband and young son in Dorset.

Margaret Cundiff has worked in the Church of England since 1973, as a lay worker, deaconess, deacon and finally priest. She also broadcasts regularly and serves as Diocesan Mothers' Union Chaplain in the York Diocese. Her most recent book for BRF is *Still Time for Eternity*.

Jane Cornish is the 2000 winner of the Shelagh Brown Memorial Prize. She has been writing group study notes for many years for her local Anglican church and is now training for local lay ministry.

David Winter is retired from parish ministry. An honorary Canon of Christ Church, Oxford, he is well known as a writer and broadcaster. His most recent book for BRF is *Old Words, New Life*. He is a Series Editor of *The People's Bible Commentary*.

David Spriggs is a Baptist minister, currently working as Head of Church Relations for Bible Society, where he had also been Project Director for The Open Book. He is the author of *Connected Christianity* (BRF, 2005).

Further BRF reading for this issue

For more in-depth coverage of some of the passages in these
Bible reading notes, we recommend the following titles:

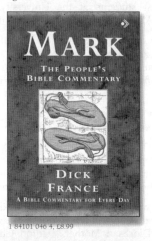

1 84101 046 4, £8.99

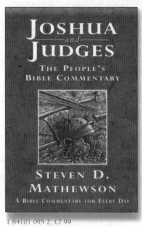

1 84101 095 2, £7.99

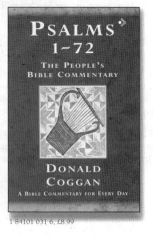

1 84101 031 6, £8.99

Naomi Starkey writes...

In some ways, September feels more like the start of the year than January, as schools begin new terms and people head back to work after summer holidays. It is around now that annoying people start to comment on just how few shopping days are left until Christmas! Tinsel seems to appear earlier every year in high street window displays, presumably to put passers-by in a suitably festive mood, prepared to pay that little bit more for a special something for that special somebody...

We have a double helping of Judges during the next four months, with John Proctor and then with Rachel Boulding. While parts of this particular book are among some of the less digestible bits of the Old Testament, we still need to read and reflect on it if we are to grow a biblically rooted faith. Judges is as much part of scripture as the cadences of the Psalms (which we visit with Jane Cornish) or the familiar Gospel narratives (see our readings on Mark 3 and 4 with Peter Graves). It is good, too, to revisit the story of somebody like Samson, whom we may not have thought about since Sunday school days. Whatever else people may say about the Bible, characters such as Samson mean that it just cannot be described as boring.

For our Christmas readings, David Spriggs explores the theme of celebration. He challenges us to think about how we can celebrate meaningfully, rejoicing in the story of Jesus' birth and enjoying time in the company of those we love. In the pressure to get Christmas 'just right'—especially if we are in charge of the shopping and catering arrangements—we can so easily forget why we are doing it in the first place. It is worth noting that BRF published David's new book *Connected Christianity* in June this year. Its focus is discovering the riches of the Old Testament and I recommend it to anybody who wants to get to grips with this part of the Bible.

Finally, I would like to say a special 'thank you and goodbye' to Margaret Cundiff, as this is her final appearance on the *New Daylight* contributor team. In this issue, she offers her personal selection of Old Testament kings, and guides us among the Jeroboams, Jehoashs and Jehoiakims with her usual blend of gentle humour and insight.

Mark 3 and 4

Written about AD65, and certainly prior to the fall of Jerusalem in AD70, ancient tradition suggests that Mark's Gospel was written in Rome by John Mark (mentioned in Acts 12:12, 15:37 and perhaps Mark 14:51). It was intended as a summary of the preaching of the apostle Peter. Deeply convinced that Jesus was the divinely appointed Messiah, Mark portrays him as constantly active. His ministry is characterized by a succession of mighty works that—to those who had eyes to see—were signs of the presence of God's power and kingdom.

Mark is the earliest and shortest of the Gospels. It is written with an obvious concern for detail and in a very vivid and urgent style. Indeed, the phrase translated 'and immediately' appears about 40 times in only 16 chapters.

The series of readings from chapters 3 and 4 that follow focus on the Galilean ministry of Jesus and the human response to it. His family wonders if he is mentally ill. The Pharisees oppose him because he is more concerned with the spirit of the Law than its minute details. The crowds, however, amazed and intrigued, listen to him gladly. Some of his followers respond happily to his call to discipleship and are willing to journey around with him and then, eventually, be sent out to proclaim the good news themselves.

Chapter 4 tells the parable of the sower. It reminds us that, just as different types of soil produce a harvest of varied quality, the human heart responds to the message of the kingdom in a whole variety of different ways. Several other parables then reflect on the experience of God's reign and the power of the gospel. Finally, as Jesus stills the storm on Galilee, we see that even the elements of nature are subject to his power and authority and he can still calm the storms in our lives, thus leading us in the ways of trust, peace and obedience.

Describing Mark as 'the Gospel for the cynic in a hurry', Dr Tom Wright says, 'Mark takes you by the scruff of the neck, and tells you breathlessly, that this is urgent and important, and you'd better listen carefully'. Certainly, from these two brief chapters, we gain much insight into who Jesus is and why we, too, must take his message seriously.

Peter Graves

7

Love, not legalism

Again he [Jesus] entered the synagogue, and a man was there who had a withered hand. They [the Pharisees] watched him to see whether he would cure him on the Sabbath, so that they might accuse him... Then he said to them, 'Is it lawful to do good or to do harm on the Sabbath, to save life or to kill?' But they were silent. He looked around at them with anger; he was grieved at their hardness of heart and said to the man, 'Stretch out your hand.' He stretched it out, and his hand was restored. The Pharisees went out and immediately conspired with the Herodians against him, how to destroy him.

At the end of the previous chapter, Mark tells how the disciples were accused of breaking Sabbath law because they plucked heads of grain as they walked through cornfields. In reply, Jesus stressed a fundamental principle: 'The Sabbath was made for humankind and not humankind for the Sabbath' (v. 27). He moves beyond the letter of the Law to its spirit and intention. It was never intended as a burden to be carried, but as an opportunity for renewal and refreshment that should carry us. Love and freedom are at the heart of true religion. It must never be reduced to the keeping of rules and scrupulous practice of ritual should not take precedence over human need.

To the Pharisees, though, Jesus was acting with reckless abandon —hence the note of conflict and controversy in today's reading. He threatened their understanding of religion as strict obedience to the Law and, in so doing, undermined their authority and status in society.

The man with the withered hand becomes a test case. They are more interested in bringing him down than helping a person in need. Jesus' response to their obstinate stupidity and closed minds is a mixture of anger and sadness.

Nowhere does Jesus water down the significance of observing the Lord's day, but he wants us to keep it in such a way that we honour God. We all need space and time for worship, rest and recreation, but even on the Sabbath it is right to do good, respond to human need and preserve life.

Prayer

Thank you, Lord, for the gift of time and space for worship and recreation. Help us to use it wisely and lovingly.

PG

Beyond superficiality

A great multitude from Galilee followed him; hearing all that he was doing, they came to him in great numbers from Judaea, Jerusalem, Idumea, beyond the Jordan, and the region around Tyre and Sidon. He told his disciples to have a boat ready for him because of the crowd, so that they would not crush him; for he had cured many, so that all who had diseases pressed upon him to touch him. Whenever the unclean spirits saw him, they fell down before him and shouted, 'You are the Son of God!' But he sternly ordered them not to make him known.

If Jesus was to have the energy to carry on his work effectively, he needed space for rest and recreation. He, too, needed a Sabbath!

We saw yesterday that he was facing opposition from the religious leaders. With the ordinary people, however, he was extremely popular. Enthusiastic crowds flocked to him—not only from Galilee but also Judah, Jerusalem and parts of what we now call Jordan and Lebanon. No wonder he asked his disciples to have a boat ready for him. He needed to avoid the crush.

At the human level, Jesus' Galilean ministry was extremely successful. His amazing teaching and healing power certainly attracted large numbers, but the people who came did not realize the significance of who he was or what he was doing. For now, only the evil spirits perceived his true identity and they did so out of fear.

Of course, Jesus wanted people to recognize him as the 'Son of God', but he knew that such language was open to a whole variety of interpretations—many of which would be inaccurate and unhelpful. Without knowledge and commitment, support for Jesus and his teaching would be superficial and inadequate. To confess Jesus as the 'Son of God' must be more than an affirmation of orthodox doctrine. It needs to be a life-transforming experience. We only really know Jesus when we become his trusting and obedient disciples. Hence, he forbids the spirits to make him known: the time was not yet right. Later, all would become clear—finally and supremely via the cross and resurrection.

Prayer

Forgive the superficiality of our faith and commitment. Help us to know, love and serve you in all things.

PG

Called and commissioned

He went up the mountain and called to him those whom he wanted, and they came to him. And he appointed twelve, whom he also named apostles, to be with him, and to be sent out to proclaim the message, and to have authority to cast out demons.

Rejected by the Pharisees, Jesus now chooses twelve disciples and, in so doing, reminds us of the twelve tribes of Israel. After the resurrection, they would become the leaders of the Church, the new Israel of God, so it is not surprising that this mountain-top experience was later regarded as their ordination as apostles.

Throughout the Bible, important encounters with God often took place on mountains and this was certainly such an occasion. As in any Christian vocation, the initiative comes from God who calls us to serve him. We have to respond to that call and then he appoints us to the office he has called us to and transforms us into the people he wants us to become.

The twelve were called 'to proclaim the message' (v. 14) and were given authority to cast out demons. As Mark frequently links healing with exorcism, we can see that they were called to set people free from all that restricted them and offer a life of wholeness. None of this would be possible unless they knew the living presence of Jesus. Their prime calling was to be with Jesus and then, out of that close companionship with the master, they were given the power to preach and heal.

Whatever our task in the Church, the most important thing is to be with Jesus. It is vital that we take time to pray and read the scriptures. Worship, fellowship and service are important 'means of grace' that can help deepen our relationship with the Lord so that we can be empowered to serve him effectively. It is all too easy to rush around being busy for God and, in so doing, lose the serenity that comes from being still and quiet in his presence. Christianity is essentially being with God. Out of that relationship comes the strength to serve.

Prayer

Teach me, Lord, to relax in your presence and be sustained by your Spirit. Help me to abide in you and you in me, that my life really will bear much fruit.

PG

Power and prejudice

And the scribes who came down from Jerusalem said, 'He has Beelzebul, and by the ruler of demons he casts out demons.' And he called them to him, and spoke to them in parables, 'How can Satan cast out Satan? If a kingdom is divided against itself, that kingdom cannot stand... And if Satan has risen up against himself and is divided, he cannot stand, but his end has come. But no one can enter a strong man's house and plunder his property without first tying up the strong man; then indeed the house can be plundered.'

The ministry of Jesus was obviously having an enormous impact on all who witnessed it. It set people thinking, and demanded a verdict. His family thought him mad and, therefore, under the influence of demons (v. 21). As he was 'beside himself', they tried to seize him. Although concerned for him, they had little understanding of his aims and purposes.

Few of us like to be disturbed or made to change established views and familiar ways. Uninformed opinion backed up by long experience can often lead to prejudice. Maybe that was the problem of the official representatives of Judaism. Although convinced of his spiritual power, the scribes were perplexed. Where did this power come from? If they admitted that it came from God, their own theology and social standing would be undermined. He must surely, then, be empowered by evil spirits instead. Thus, we find them using their skill with words to reinforce prejudice rather than face the challenge of the gospel.

Jesus argues that the devil produces disease and falsehood, whereas he removes them. If his activity were due to satanic influence, then the devil would be pursuing two directly conflicting policies at the same time. Such an internal 'civil war' would be absurd.

His next parable is based on the proverbial saying that you cannot rob a strong man unless you have first overpowered and restrained him. If, as a result of his exorcisms and healing, Jesus has robbed Satan of his control over the sick, then Satan has been 'bound' by one even stronger than himself, so, obviously, Jesus is empowered by God alone.

Sunday prayer

As I worship today, Lord, take away the prejudice that blinds me to the truth and help me to be open to the challenge of your word.

PG

The unforgivable sin

'Truly I tell you, people will be forgiven for their sins and whatever blasphemies they utter; but whoever blasphemes against the Holy Spirit can never have forgiveness, but is guilty of an eternal sin'— for they had said, 'He has an unclean spirit.'

Rabbis often declared that certain sins were so terrible that those who committed them could 'have no part in the world to come'. For Jesus, the one unforgivable sin is 'blasphemy against the Holy Spirit'. To avoid any misunderstanding, we need to read these verses in the light of the passage we considered yesterday.

All the evidence points to the fact that the ministry of Jesus was empowered by the Holy Spirit of God. By refusing to recognize his saving work for what it was— attributing it instead to Satan—the scribes were cutting themselves off from the possibility of salvation. They recognized God at work, but then called such work evil or unclean. Such 'blasphemy against the Holy Spirit' is the most extreme form of opposition to God. It so identifies with the kingdom of evil that all virtues are reversed. Good becomes evil, ugliness beauty and falsehood becomes truth.

The scribes' offence is not that they did not understand, nor that they asked questions, but their resolute rejection of the truth. They had seen grace in action and ascribed it to the evil one. In the original Greek, the imperfect tense is used—'they were saying'— which implies continuous or habitual action. As theirs was a fixed position—a firm decision of deliberate rejection—forgiveness would not be possible. After all, with such an attitude, they would be unable to seek it.

Unfortunately, this passage has led many to feel very guilty and wonder if they have committed the 'unforgivable sin'. The good news is that if we are concerned about our guilt, we cannot possibly be guilty of a deliberate and obstinate rejection of the Holy Spirit. Only those who resolutely set themselves against the goodness of God and the reality of his forgiveness are excluded from it.

Prayer

Transform my guilty fear, Lord, into the assurance of your acceptance, love and forgiveness. Open my heart to your truth and, by your Holy Spirit, mould me into the likeness of Jesus.

PG

The family of God

Then his mother and his brothers came; and standing outside, they sent to him and called him. A crowd was sitting around him; and they said to him, 'Your mother and your brothers and sisters are outside, asking for you.' And he replied, 'Who are my mother and my brothers?' And looking at those who sat around him, he said, 'Here are my mother and my brothers! Whoever does the will of God is my brother and sister and mother.'

Earlier (v. 21), we find the family of Jesus trying to draw him away from public ministry. They did not recognize that, empowered by the Holy Spirit, he was doing the work of God. Now the family appears again and he seems to reject them. As family life was tremendously important in that culture and time, these words from Jesus would have shocked his hearers. Children who neglected their responsibilities to their parents flouted the commandments of God. Why, then, does Jesus seemingly undermine the importance of the family when all law-abiding Jews saw themselves as having a primary obligation to it?

To answer this question we need to see that the focus of these verses shifts from the blood relations of Jesus to the calling of his hearers. He does not want to water down the importance of family life—he wants to enlarge our vision of it. Ties stronger than blood were being forged. With the dawning of the kingdom of God came a new kind of family, consisting of all who responded to his message and sought to do God's will.

This message would have had enormous relevance to the early Christians, and it certainly speaks to us today, too. Entry into the kingdom is not based on ancestry or privilege, but on faith, trust and obedience. Regardless of opposition from family, friends or Jewish religious leaders, every disciple had entered a new family—the Church. Jesus was not a distant king ruling the world from a throne far away, but dwelt among us as our brother, sharing his love and truth. He still calls us to be the family of God and, through obedient service, share in his ongoing ministry.

Reflection

He bids us build each other up;
And gathered into one,
To our high calling's glorious hope
We hand in hand go on.

Charles Wesley (1707–88)
PG

13

The parable of the sower

'Listen! A sower went out to sow. And as he sowed, some seed fell on the path, and the birds came and ate it up. Other seed fell on rocky ground, where it did not have much soil, and it sprang up quickly, since it had no depth of soil. And when the sun rose, it was scorched; and since it had no root, it withered away. Other seed fell among thorns, and the thorns grew up and choked it, and it yielded no grain. Other seed fell into good soil and brought forth grain, growing up and increasing and yielding 30 and 60 and a hundredfold.'

A young missionary was reading this passage to a Spanish-speaking congregation in South America. When he spoke of the seed in the good soil, the congregation audibly gasped. After the service he sought an explanation. His congregation had been amazed at the enormity of the harvest. These peasant farmers were used to poor soil and had never experienced such an abundant yield. Maybe they had a better understanding of the parable than we do. They certainly realized that the state of the soil was crucial to the quality of the harvest.

Some years ago, I visited the Methodist Church in Sarawak on the island of Borneo. What most impressed me was the youthfulness and enthusiasm of church leaders. They were committed to Christ, convinced of the power and relevance of their message and determined to share their faith with others. Of course they had problems to overcome, but they saw them as opportunities for growth and tackled them with expectant faith.

In the West, we are so often troubled by the difficulty of sharing the gospel that we lose sight of those who are willing to respond. We all know that when the word is proclaimed, the birds of cynicism and secularism can stop it taking root. Like seed on rocky soil, the response of some is too shallow for it to last. Some are lured by material things and choked by the thorns of scepticism. Despite all these things, this parable encourages us to sow faithfully, knowing that the harvest will come. It also challenges us to be the kind of soil from which God can reap a mighty harvest.

Prayer

Teach me to trust you, Lord, and help me to serve you faithfully.

PG

Understanding the parables

When he was alone, those who were around him along with the 12 asked him about the parables. And he said to them, 'To you has been given the secret of the kingdom of God, but for those outside, everything comes in parables; in order that "they may indeed look, but not perceive, and may indeed listen, but not understand; so that they may not turn again and be forgiven."'

Jesus is speaking with his inner core of followers who are wrestling with a big problem. They could see the 'kingdom of God' at work in and through him, but why were so many unable to respond? Jesus reminds them that it is only because God has revealed the secret to them, that they can understand the significance of his life and ministry. The parables enabled them to grasp the mystery, make the story their own and become a part of it.

What, then, was the point of the parables for those who did not realize that, in the ministry of Jesus, God was at work among them? Jesus replies by quoting Isaiah 6:9–10: a riddle that is difficult for us to understand. After a moving account of Isaiah's call to prophetic ministry, we find these puzzling verses, which imply that the prophet must preach 'in order that' the people will not respond. In using the same words, Jesus gives the impression that he does not want his hearers to understand and believe.

The equivalent passage in Matthew (13:10–16) is more helpful. It suggests that Jesus uses parables because, due to their hardness of heart, they will not grasp his message without them: 'For this people's heart has grown dull, and their ears are hard of hearing, and they have shut their eyes; so that they might… understand with their heart and turn—and I would heal them' (v. 15, quoting Isaiah again). Although people may not understand the parables initially, they are still a powerful means of communication. Their ultimate purpose is to set us thinking and encourage us to explore the gospel message revealed by them. Then, as we hear, believe and act on the words of Jesus, we grasp the secret of the kingdom of God.

Prayer

Enable me to understand your truth, Lord, and help me to do your perfect will.

PG

15

Ears to hear

He said to them [the disciples], 'Is a lamp brought in to be put under the bushel basket, or under the bed and not on the lampstand? For there is nothing hidden, except to be disclosed; nor is anything secret, except to come to light. Let anyone with ears to hear listen!' And he said to them, 'Pay attention to what you hear; the measure you give will be the measure you get, and still more will be given you. For to those who have, more will be given; and from those who have nothing, even what they have will be taken away.'

Although during our Lord's lifetime the parables may have concealed the truths of the kingdom for unbelievers, this was not their ultimate purpose. After the resurrection, all would be disclosed and the message widely proclaimed. Just as a lamp is meant to give light, so the parables are meant to be understood. Nothing remains hidden forever. The mystery of the kingdom, which only God can reveal, is now seen in Jesus. We must therefore pay careful attention to the example of his life and the depth of his teaching.

The need to listen and respond is the central thrust of Mark 4. In referring to the 'measure you give' and 'get' (v. 24), he is probably quoting a contemporary proverb that reflected the conditions of the ancient Near East. The rich and powerful constantly received gifts, whereas the poor and those lacking influence were likely to be cheated. Thus, those who do have

spiritual insight will have it enlarged and those who do not will be led into even more ignorance and bewilderment. The more we listen, the more we discover.

Lazy or indifferent listeners, however, are warned that if they do not keep seeking and discovering, they will find their capacity for hearing lessened. Indeed, all that they have learned will soon be forgotten.

Jesus expects us to respond to his teaching with serious and persistent faith, trust and obedience. The encouraging news is that, when we do so respond, more will be revealed and we shall go on discovering the riches of his grace.

Reflection

For more we ask; we open then
Our hearts to embrace thy will:
Turn, and revive us, Lord, again,
With all thy fullness fill.

Charles Wesley (1707–88)

PG

The seed growing secretly

He also said, 'The kingdom of God is as if someone would scatter seed on the ground, and would sleep and rise night and day, and the seed would sprout and grow, he does not know how. The earth produces of itself, first the stalk, then the head, then the full grain in the head. But when the grain is ripe, at once he goes in with his sickle, because the harvest has come.'

After a wedding ceremony, I was asked to join the bride and groom for a photograph. As I stood there, a seeming stranger came and greeted me warmly. I recognized him when he said, 'It's ages since we last met'. Forty years ago Howard came to London to study music. He lodged with a member of our church, joined our young people's Bible class and often worshipped with us. We spoke of the people we had known then. Both of us bore testimony to the ways in which their faith and life had influenced and inspired us. Many have now gone to heaven, but the power of their example lives on. The seeds they planted had born fruit in the lives of so many of our contemporaries— not least in our own. Thanks to the secret work of the Holy Spirit nurturing those seeds, their faithfulness had yielded a rich harvest.

The ministry of Jesus had met with hindrance and opposition. It had not yet produced spectacular results, but the seeds had been sown. God would bring forth the harvest—especially after the resurrection. There was no need to despair.

Such a message would have been a great encouragement to the leaders of the early Church. Preaching against a background of persecution, their ministry may not have been as successful as they might have hoped, but they should not be discouraged. The success of the kingdom is not dependent on human activity alone. It is like a seed, pregnant, mysterious and fruitful, that grows independently of human effort. Thanks to the secret work of the Holy Spirit, growth and change take place even while we sleep. Our task is to witness faithfully, serve lovingly and prayerfully trust in God for the outcome.

Prayer

Help me to not take myself too seriously, Lord. Keep me obediently serving and help me to trust you for the harvest.

PG

The mustard seed

He also said, 'With what can we compare the kingdom of God, or what parable will we use for it? It is like a mustard seed, which, when sown upon the ground, is the smallest of all the seeds on earth; yet when it is sown it grows up and becomes the greatest of all shrubs, and puts forth large branches, so that the birds of the air can make nests in its shade.'

The focus of this parable is the contrast between inconspicuous beginnings and mighty outcomes. Such a contrast struck me vividly as I wandered round the ruins of ancient Ephesus, now a part of Turkey. To see so many magnificent buildings dating back to New Testament times was an inspiration. As I marvelled at the long-standing tradition of Judaism, the political power of Rome and the cultural genius of Greece, I realized how insignificant those early followers of Jesus must have seemed.

I pictured Paul with a small band of followers witnessing in the marketplace and preaching in the theatre. All the odds were against them. In the eyes of the world, they were of no consequence. They came from a variety of tribes and peoples. Few had much education. Many were slaves. Hardly any had money, power or influence. Yet, to God, these were the people chosen to further the work of the kingdom. The outcome of their faithfulness was greater than could ever have been imagined. Just as small mustard seeds could develop into shrubs large enough for the birds to rest in their shade, so from small beginnings came the great movement that we call the Christian Church.

All over the world, too, there are works of God that have come from seemingly insignificant origins. Churches, charities, schools and hospitals were often founded by a few people who caught a vision and then worked hard to turn their dreams into reality. The same is often true of movements working for political change. Think, for example, of how much the civil rights movement in America owes to the Christian vision of Martin Luther King. When faith is weak, the work hard and the impact small, remember the mustard seed, and be encouraged!

Sunday prayer

Encourage us by the example of the mustard seed, Lord. Keep us faithful, especially in small things.

PG

MARK 4:37–41 (NRSV)

The stilling of the storm

A great gale arose, and the waves beat into the boat, so that the boat was already being swamped. But he was in the stern, asleep on the cushion; and they woke him up and said to him, 'Teacher, do you not care that we are perishing?' He woke up and rebuked the wind, and said to the sea, 'Peace! Be still!' Then the wind ceased, and there was a dead calm. He said to them, 'Why are you afraid? Have you still no faith?' And they were filled with great awe and said to one another, 'Who then is this, that even the wind and the sea obey him?'

In 1948, the World Council of Churches was inaugurated in Amsterdam. As its logo, it adopted an early Christian symbol—a storm-tossed boat with a cross for a mast.

Today's reading describes a miracle performed by Jesus on Lake Galilee. Mark, the Gospel's author, was using this story to foster trust in the early Church. He wanted them to see that Jesus would be with them in their hour of need.

The story is full of profound symbolism. The boat had become a symbol of the Church. The stormy waters represented the realm of evil. Just a year or so before this Gospel was written, Emperor Nero had begun persecuting Christians. The question 'Do you not care that we are perishing?' would have reflected the panic and fear that must have been experienced by those who first heard it. There would have been much joy as they heard Jesus say 'Peace! Be still'. The power of Jesus was triumphing over a hostile world, overcoming the realm of evil and conquering the fear of death. Not only was Jesus the Lord of nature and history, but the peace of his presence quelled their anxious fear.

In Rembrandt's painting *The Calming of the Sea*, the artist has painted an extra disciple in the boat. He has the face of Rembrandt himself. We are all in the boat with Jesus. Left to ourselves, the storms may overwhelm us, but when we seek the help of Jesus, strength, courage and serenity will be ours.

Reflection

The storm may roar without me,
my heart may low be laid;
But God is round about me,
and can I be dismayed?

Anna L. Waring (1823–1910)

PG

Judges 6—11

Gideon and Jephthah conquered kingdoms by faith and administered justice, says the letter to the Hebrews (11:32–33) in the New Testament over 1000 years after the days of the book of Judges. Judges is full of faith, but again and again it is flawed faith, fragile faith, struggling to find a way through rough times. God was present, but the people's trust in God was patchy and erratic. The results were an unpredictable blend of triumph and tragedy. Judges is not a comfortable read.

The date is roughly 1100BC. The place is the Holy Land—Israel, the West Bank and Jordan on today's map. The people are the tribes of Israel. They have come through the desert and found a footing in the Promised Land. Now they have to organize their lives, defend themselves against well-armed neighbours and, through it all, grow in faith and trust God as the key player in their community.

There was as yet no king of this nation and leaders emerged in very varied ways. Sometimes God called a person to serve, while at other times people schemed their way into the top positions. In both cases, there were jealousies to contend with—people who doubted the leader, who thought they could do better themselves. These were pressured times and pressure does not always draw out the best in human nature. It can deepen our faith, but it may also magnify our faults.

The story is complicated and we shall dip into a little of it each day. The snippets we choose should give a sense of how the plot and characters develop, but you may still want to read all of these chapters through from beginning to end, if you find you have a quiet half-hour. Chapters 6—8 on Gideon will take us through the first week and chapters 9—11 on Abimelech and Jephthah the second week.

This dark and difficult corner of the Old Testament tells of distant and troubled times, but they are still part of God's story of grace and our heritage of faith. In some ways we know better than the people did then. Yet we surely have gaps and blind spots in our understanding of God, too. So, when you read in Judges about flawed faith, also note that there are places telling of a God who loves—who loves Gideon, Jephthah, you and me, flaws and faith and all.

John Proctor

JUDGES 6:1–6, 11–15 (NRSV, ABRIDGED)

Discretion and valour

The Israelites did... evil in the sight of the Lord, and the Lord gave them into the hand of Midian for seven years... The Midianites... would encamp against them and destroy the produce of the land... and the Israelites cried out to the Lord for help... Now the angel of the Lord came... as... Gideon was beating out wheat in the wine press, to hide it from the Midianites... and said to him, 'The Lord is with you, you mighty warrior... Go in this might of yours and deliver Israel...' He responded, 'But sir... My clan is the weakest in Manasseh, and I am the least in my family.'

The plotline of Judges has a repeated pattern: the people sin and enemies come in; God raises up a leader and the enemy is driven out; then the land has rest for a while, until it all starts over again. This is a vital point in this cycle—God is finding the right leader. As so often, God chooses unexpected people—younger brothers, fearful prophets, untaught disciples. Deborah (Judges 4 and 5) was a female leader in a rough male world and Gideon, too, seems to be plucked from the back of the queue—not the person his neighbours would have picked as team captain.

When it comes to potential, we tend to judge on past record and present ability, but God reads people on the inside and looks to what they might become. Faith and grace and the following wind of the Spirit can open up wide possibilities for service. God's call often reaches much further than we would expect.

Gideon was keeping his head down, quite literally—his next year's food supply depended on him doing just that. God, however, wanted him to raise his sights to what his land might be like if it were free and the people had no need to hide or fear. Then Gideon had questions, even excuses—just as Moses had before him (Exodus 3 and 4)—but this was God's time to raise up a new Moses, one who would know from the start that real power and purpose belong to God. It would not do to call a proud leader. That might spoil everything.

Prayer

God of grace and gift, when you beckon me to new service, may I respond with faith, yet without pride.

JP

No place like home

Then Gideon perceived that it was the angel of the Lord... Then Gideon built an altar there to the Lord, and called it, The Lord is peace... That night the Lord said to him, 'Take your father's bull... and pull down the altar of Baal that belongs to your father, and cut down the sacred pole that is beside it... then take the... bull, and offer it as a burnt offering with the wood of the sacred pole...' So Gideon took ten of his servants, and did as the Lord had told him; but because he was afraid of his family and the townspeople to do it by day, he did it by night.

Any sort of encounter with God is a stirring experience, but you still have to go home afterwards. Will the family notice? Should you tell friends? Will anyone be convinced? Gideon had been called to lead. Where would he start?

He had started with worship. He called his altar 'The Lord is peace'. The Lord is 'shalom'—our welfare, well-being, security and true prosperity. These were days of many gods and lords. Gideon's neighbours knew well the names of Baal and Asherah—the nature-god and goddess of the surrounding Canaanite peoples. In such multicultural times, one might wonder where best to invest faith and trust. Indeed, Gideon's father maintained an altar to Baal and a wooden pillar to Asherah, but Gideon was making a statement: 'I trust Yahweh, the God of Israel'.

Then the Lord pushed him on, beyond this gesture of personal commitment, to a strong bid for the loyalty of others. Even at night this was a bold venture, to wreck the family shrine and sacrifice a prize bull in the flames. Fortunately, Gideon's father stood up for him (v. 31). Gideon had won his respect—grudging respect perhaps, but support, too. The encounter with God was making a difference at home. Gideon's call to lead was starting to take effect.

The Hebrew name Gideon means 'hacker' or 'tree feller', so was it really a sort of nickname, forever recalling this one night-time episode? This was a turning point in his life. He had taken a big risk at home and would now be ready for greater challenges ahead.

Prayer

God, give me wisdom, patience and courage, as I live for you among people who know me well.

JP

JUDGES 6:33–37 (NRSV, ABRIDGED)

The dry run

Then all the Midianites and the Amalekites and the people of the east came together, and crossing the Jordan they encamped in the Valley of Jezreel. But the spirit of the Lord took possession of Gideon; and he sounded the trumpet... Then Gideon said to God, 'In order to see whether you will deliver Israel by my hand, as you have said, I am going to lay a fleece of wool on the threshing-floor; if there is dew on the fleece alone, and it is dry on all the ground, then I shall know.'

The time for action had come. The enemy were moving west, towards the heartland of Gideon's tribe and clan, but God was on the move, too, stirring Gideon to new boldness and resolve. Several of the judges were touched by God's Spirit—Othniel (3:10), Jephthah (11:29), Samson (13:25)—but only of Gideon is it said that the Spirit 'took possession' of him (v. 34). It is interesting that 'clothed him' is the Hebrew word used here, as if he were wrapped around with the power and presence of God.

God's spirit is magnetic. People are drawn. Gideon had the confidence and conviction to summon an army, and men came to join him from his own tribe and from further afield (v. 35). The trumpet blast was a signal to gather, to meet force with force, invasion with defence. The reader expects to hear the clash of arms, but then suddenly comes a pause and we see

Gideon as a man alone. Outwardly he has been confident; inwardly he wants a fresh sign that God is with him.

So, Gideon puts a fleece out over two nights. The first morning he finds the fleece wet and the ground dry (vv. 36–38) and the second time the opposite happens (vv. 39–40). Twice over God has answered, exactly as Gideon asked. This experiment seems to be a stepping stone, a way of advancing in faith in order to face the coming challenge. Testing God is a tricky business, of course. We are told not to push the limits (Luke 4:12), but special times create special needs. Gideon needed assurance and God was ready to give it.

Reflection

How do you deal with God when there are challenges ahead? What strengthens your faith and gives you perspective on the situation?

JP

Watered down

The Lord said to Gideon, 'The troops with you are too many for me to give the Midianites into their hand. Israel would only take the credit away from me, saying, "My own hand has delivered me." … therefore proclaim… "Whoever is fearful… let him return home".' … 22,000 returned, and 10,000 remained. Then the Lord said… '…take them down to the water… All those who lap the water with their tongues, as a dog laps, you shall put to one side; all those who kneel down to drink, putting their hands to their mouths… put to the other side.' The number of those that lapped was 300… So he [Gideon]… sent all the rest of Israel back to their own tents.

It is hard to work out how this water test operated. Did some men crouch down for a few seconds to gather water in their cupped hands, while others sank their faces into the stream? That might pick out the most vigilant of the soldiers or the hardiest or… no one really knows. The main point of the test is to reduce the number in Gideon's army. There are two reasons for this.

The first is tactical. A small force will be needed for a surprise attack. Gideon is already forming a plan involving jars and trumpets, as we shall see in tomorrow's reading. The second and more important reason has to do with God. This will be God's battle. A victory will do little good if the people think that they have won it themselves. A large army might take pride in their own strength. A small force is much more likely to remember how vulnerable they were and how much they depended on God for everything to work out right.

This curious drinking test is part of a divine strategy. It is all of a piece with God's call of Gideon. An unlikely leader, from one of the smaller clans and now a tiny army—no one will doubt that the power has come from God.

Reflection and prayer

If God puts us through experiences that make us feel small, it is not to take our confidence away, but to focus it in faith and prayer. Even when we are small, God is great. 'My grace is sufficient for you, for power is made perfect in weakness' (2 Corinthians 12:9).

JP

Sound bites

There was a man telling a dream to his comrade… '… a cake of barley bread tumbled into the camp of Midian, and came to the tent, and struck it so that it fell…' And his comrade answered, 'This is… the sword of Gideon…' When Gideon heard… the dream… he worshipped; and he returned to the camp of Israel, and said, 'Get up; for the Lord has given the army of Midian into your hand.' After he divided the three hundred men into three companies, and put trumpets into the hands of all of them, and empty jars, with torches inside… he said… '… When I blow the trumpet… you also blow… and shout, "For the Lord and for Gideon!"'

The story has trailed Gideon, very quietly, to the fringe of the enemy camp, where he overhears a strange dream. He has been fearful (v. 10), but so are the Midianites. For all their force, they are on unknown territory and they sleep uneasily, wondering what is out there in the dark. Gideon's reputation is growing and so is his confidence. God has given him another sign. This is the moment to put his plan into action.

The Israelites move silently, their torches covered by jars to keep the flame down and shield the light. They approach the enemy lines from three sides. Then suddenly they blast their trumpets, smash their jars and fill the night with flares. The effect is chaotic. The enemy soldiers strike out aimlessly in the dark, landing blows on each other. They run while Gideon's men stand still (vv. 21–22). They scatter and do not stop.

Why did it work so well? Surprise helped, obviously. The darkness helped, too, as did nerve, on the part of Gideon and his men, and faith, that God was in it. Above all, God himself helped. Every victory in Judges is part of a cycle of rescue and restoration. God was bringing his people back, through faith to freedom. When Deborah and Barak won a battle, they sang, 'Lord… you marched' (5:4) and here, too, the Lord was surely tiptoeing through the darkness beside the leader he had called to achieve so much more than anyone expected (Ephesians 3:20). To God be the glory.

Prayer

Lord, please help me to trace your hand of rescue in my own experiences.

JP

Tense and tired

Then Gideon came to the Jordan and crossed over, he and the 300 who were with him, exhausted and famished. So he said to the people of Succoth, 'Please give some loaves of bread to my followers, for they are exhausted, and I am pursuing Zebah and Zalmunna, the kings of Midian.' But the officials of Succoth said, 'Do you already have in your possession the hands of Zebah and Zalmunna, that we should give bread to your army?' Gideon replied, 'Well then, when the Lord has given Zebah and Zalmunna into my hand, I will trample your flesh on the thorns of the wilderness and briers.'

This passage gives a very ugly taste to the story. War is unpleasant at best, but there has also been something noble about the defensive war that Gideon has led. He has protected his people, grown in faith, and given the Midianites a taste of their own medicine. Now we see a new side of his character—not the boldness of belief, but the anger of revenge.

Gideon was in hot pursuit. Succoth was beyond the river Jordan, 50 miles from the battle. It was an Israelite town and Gideon claimed help there. It was also vulnerable, exposed to invasion from the desert, and knowing that Midian was a difficult neighbour. Little wonder, then, that the men of Succoth were cautious. Had Gideon really beaten the Midianites? Would it not be wiser to wait and see who finally came out on top?

Gideon had once been hesitant himself, but now he has no patience with the doubters of Succoth. He meets caution with cruelty, essentially saying 'Let them see who is boss' (vv. 13–17). This is a hero to fear, but no longer one to love easily.

People can change suddenly and not always for the better. New experiences bring out unseen sides of our personality. Danger or tiredness can irritate us. The relief of coming through a tense moment may close our eyes to the stresses and fears in other people. Gideon has won a battle, with the help of God's Spirit. Living by the Spirit (Galatians 5:16) might be more difficult, however. That requires patience and self-control.

Sunday prayer

Lord, when life jolts and strains and tests us, help us to respond in ways that honour you.

JP

JUDGES 8:22–27, 30–32 (NRSV, ABRIDGED)

Going the distance

Then the Israelites said to Gideon, 'Rule over us, you and your son and your grandson also; for you have delivered us out of the hand of Midian.' Gideon said to them, 'I will not rule over you, and my son will not rule over you; the Lord will rule over you... each of you give me an earring he has taken as booty.' ... The weight of the golden earrings... was 1700 shekels of gold (apart from the crescents and the pendants and the purple garments...). Gideon made an ephod of it and put it in his town, in Ophrah... and it became a snare... Now Gideon had 70 sons... Then Gideon... died at a good old age.

Yesterday's reading showed how pressure can affect a person's character. Today, we see how popularity can turn a head and a heart. Successful generals often find their way into politics and some make a reasonable job of it. Gideon has risen swiftly from farm to fame and has to find his spiritual balance again while coping with the giddy heights of public acclaim. It seems that he never really succeeds.

Gideon's first response sounds fine—solid religious affirmation: 'The Lord is in charge here'—yet the claims of the Lord are tamed in ways that highlight Gideon's own position. The spoils of war are made into a splendid priestly garment, to be kept at Ophrah, Gideon's home town. There the people will worship their invisible God and Gideon will have a very visible symbol of power. You can almost hear the lowing of Aaron's golden calf (Exodus 32:1–6).

So, Gideon's story comes full circle. From offering worship at Ophrah (6:24), to securing his position by means of worship at Ophrah (8:27). From the least in the clan, to a father of many. Through it all, though, God seems to become more remote. Had that first encounter with the angel stuck in Gideon's memory or had the flames of faith burnt down to an ember, as if covered by an earthen jar?

Reflection

Many Christians find that the enthusiasms of new faith alter with the years. Styles change, but substance need not. We are called to a long faithfulness, to shine with the steady light of Christ, as we travel towards the inheritance that will never fade (1 Peter 1:4).

JP

Power play

Now Abimelech... went to Shechem to his mother's kinsfolk and said to them... 'Which is better... that all 70 of the sons of Jerubbaal rule over you, or that one rule over you?' ... They gave him 70 pieces of silver out of the temple of Baal-berith with which Abimelech hired worthless and reckless fellows... He went to his father's house at Ophrah, and killed his brothers... 70 men, on one stone; but Jotham, the youngest son of Jerubbaal, survived, for he hid himself. Then all the lords of Shechem... came together, and... made Abimelech king.

The story of Gideon is over, and Judges 9 tells of the unhappy legacy he left. God seems a distant figure, rarely mentioned, and honoured by almost nobody. This is a chapter of feuds, fighting and folly. Good faith, in any sense of the words, scarcely figures at all, for grudges are being worked out. People have insults to get out of their system, positions to secure and advantage to gain. The power vacuum left by Gideon's death must be filled. It wouldn't do to involve God in the action.

'Jerubbaal' (vv. 1 and 2) was an alternative name for Gideon. Abimelech was his son, but a fringe member of the family as his mother had never been given full status as Gideon's wife (8:31). Shechem was an important town in Israelite territory, but with its own ambitions, so when Abimelech put his bloody scheme to the men of Shechem, he found a ready hearing: why should they let Gideon's whole brood cling on to power? They even had money to pay for the dirty work to be done.

Abimelech hires a posse of hard men to get his half-brothers killed. It is a brutal strategy, and must have required both surprise and deceit, but it clears the way for Shechem to assert its rights and Abimelech to rule there. Perhaps the town and its new king will be able to extend their power, now that so many rivals are out of the way. The reader suspects that they will not find each other easy partners, however, as their alliance has too much blood on it already.

Reflection

How do you deal with grudges and resentment to stop them escalating? Are you carrying any bitterness that you need God's help to sort out? Can you ask for that help today?

JP

Stirring story

Jotham… cried aloud… 'Listen to me, you lords of Shechem… The trees once went out to anoint a king… So they said to the olive tree, "Reign over us." The olive tree answered them, "Shall I stop producing my rich oil by which gods and mortals are honoured, and go to sway over the trees?" … So all the trees said to the bramble, "You come and reign over us." And the bramble said… "If in good faith you are anointing me king over you, then come and take refuge in my shade; but if not, let fire come out of the bramble and devour the cedars of Lebanon."'

Jotham stands on a hill above Shechem and calls to the town below. This story is a parable, with a pointed meaning just beneath the surface. The trees try three candidates for kingship—olive, fig and vine. They all turn the job down, for all have good work to do already. The bramble appears as a last, unlikely, thought—a wild card of a nomination. His response shows how strange an idea this is: 'If you really mean this, I'll give you all the shelter I can. But if you don't, you'll find me a fiery character.'

The target of the story is Abimelech. He is the human bramble. The olive, fig and vine are just staging posts in the story, to make the point that Abimelech was the worst sort of man to be king, for the bramble is a useless plant with a chaotic, unruly pattern of growth. It affords no real shelter and can burst quickly and danger-ously into flame. This is Abimelech—a wild, unpredictable man, with no reliable gifts of care or leadership, as much of a hazard to his friends as to enemies.

Of course Jotham too is stirring up a fire, sprinkling little sparks of distrust over Shechem, but his story still carries a warning. Wrong friends can be as much trouble as enemies. What do we look for in our friends? Jotham put it like this: 'Can you find real shelter in this friendship? And is this person a fire hazard?' (compare Proverbs 26:18–21).

Prayer

Lord, help me to be a good friend, to find true friends, to put my trust in the right places and the right people.

JP

Justice from above

Abimelech was told that all the lords of the Tower of Shechem were gathered together. So Abimelech... and all the troops that were with him... cut down... brushwood... and they set the stronghold on fire... so that all the people of the Tower of Shechem... died, about 1000 men and women. Then Abimelech went to Thebez... But there was a strong tower within the city, and all the men and women... shut themselves in... Abimelech came... to burn it with fire. But a certain woman threw an upper millstone on Abimelech's head, and crushed his skull... Thus God repaid Abimelech for... killing his 70 brothers; and God also made all the wickedness of the people of Shechem fall back on their heads, and on them came the curse of Jotham.

The tale that winds through Judges 9 tells of bitter dispute between Abimelech and Shechem. Prince and people had wed in blood and could not live in peace. Eventually, Abimelech gains the upper hand and today's verses describe his attempt to stamp out the last traces of opposition. He has resorted to mass murder once and obviously has the stomach to do so again. Men, women, maybe children, too—who cares? It has become a habit.

Thebez must have sided with Shechem against Abimelech. It was about ten miles away and next in line to be wiped out. The reader expects a repeat of the previous scene, until an unnamed woman becomes heroine for the day with a shot that is as well aimed as Jotham's little parable had been. The destroyer is destroyed, the bramble crushed. The man who slew his brothers on a stone is struck by a stone. The land might now breathe again and hope for peace.

It was a woman's doing, as so often in Judges—we have had Deborah the prophetess, Jael of the milk and tent peg and now a direct hit from the top of the tower. There are strong female characters at large and later we shall see another, though in a very different role. It was God's doing, too, says the text. Justice always catches up in the end.

Reflection

One writer reckons the message of this chapter is about human relationships. Despise family ties and you will never find anything to put in their place—only anarchy. Do you agree?

JP

Swings and slide

After Abimelech, Tola son of Puah... rose to deliver Israel. He judged Israel for 23 years. Then he died, and was buried... After him came Jair the Gileadite, who judged Israel for 22 years. He had 30 sons who rode on 30 donkeys; and they had 30 towns... in the land of Gilead... Jair died, and was buried... The Israelites again did what was evil in the sight of the Lord... and he sold them into the hand of the Philistines and... the Ammonites... So the Israelites cried to the Lord, saying, 'We have sinned...' ... So they put away the foreign gods from among them and worshipped the Lord; and he could no longer bear to see Israel suffer.

Tola and Jair have been called 'minor judges'. The story gives the merest outline of their lives and work, except to say that they brought some stability to the people. After Abimelech's chaotic years (9:22ff), Tola 'rose to deliver Israel' (10:1). His task was sorting out and settling the situation, bringing peace and trust back into public life. Jair, too, seems to have had an orderly career. The sons, donkeys and towns mark him out as a prosperous man. The impression is of a period without major crisis.

Then the pendulum pattern of Judges reappears: away from God, back to God; into the hands of enemies, out of the hands of enemies. Each time, the situation becomes more tangled than before. Gideon saved Israel, but handed on a terrible legacy of ill-feeling. The next rescuer who appears will also leave memories of hurt and pain behind him, for Judges portrays not only a pendulum movement to and fro but also a gradual downward slide into unhappiness and disorder.

The constant positive, however, is God—patient, gracious and purposeful. Indeed, the last line of today's reading speaks of God's hurt and care. The Hebrew words are difficult to translate into English, but they hint at a God who bears our sins and sorrows, whose face we see most clearly on the cross. Indeed, few portions of the Old Testament anticipate the cross as profoundly as the chapter ahead—the wretched combination of faith and folly that is the story of Jephthah.

Prayer

Lord, when we pass through bad times, help us to trust you as the great and constant positive in our lives and in the world.

JP

Odd man in

Now Jephthah… the son of a prostitute, was a mighty warrior. Gilead was the father of Jephthah. Gilead's wife also bore him sons; and when his wife's sons grew up, they drove Jephthah away… Outlaws collected around Jephthah and went raiding with him… when the Ammonites made war against Israel, the elders of Gilead went to… Jephthah… They said… 'Come and be our commander, so that we may fight with the Ammonites.' But Jephthah said… 'Are you not the very ones who rejected me and drove me out of my father's house? So why do you come to me now when you are in trouble? … If you bring me home again to fight with the Ammonites, and the Lord gives them over to me, I will be your head.'

This is like the start of the story of Abimelech—one father, different mothers and men who grow up jealous and suspicious of each other. Jephthah gets no share in any family land and ends up as a man apart, on the edge of normal society. He pursues his fortune where he may, keeps one step ahead of trouble and learns how to fight.

When we think of Abimelech's story, we expect blood to be shed. This time, things take a different tack. Jephthah's kinsmen come looking for him. They are in danger and they want a fighter, someone who knows how to look after himself in a tight corner.

Jephthah drives a hard bargain. 'Be our commander', was the invitation—head the army, win the battle, then step back into the shadows—but he asks for more—to be their 'head'. If Jephthah wins the war, he will be ruler over the men who drove him away. It can hardly have been a comforting prospect for them, but desperate times create desperate actions and Jephthah has dictated his own terms. He is clever with words, as well as a sword.

So, the deal is struck, but it is only a deal, not a healing. These have not been words of forgiveness and reconciliation, but of pressing for advantage and opening of old wounds. Jephthah has been brought back in, but he is still a man alone. Nevertheless, we suspect, he is an awkward, insecure character.

Prayer

Lord, when human relationships make me feel insecure, help me find true security in you.

JP

JUDGES 11:29–34 (NRSV, ABRIDGED)

Words that come home

Then the spirit of the Lord came upon Jephthah, and he passed through Gilead and... on to the Ammonites. And Jephthah made a vow to the Lord, and said, 'If you will give the Ammonites into my hand, then whoever comes out of the doors of my house to meet me, when I return victorious from the Ammonites, shall be the Lord's, to be offered up by me as a burnt offering.' So Jephthah crossed over to the Ammonites to fight against them; and the Lord gave them into his hand... Then Jephthah came to his home... and there was his daughter coming out to meet him with timbrels and with dancing. She was his only child.

This vow was so stupid and unnecessary. Here is Jephthah the wordsmith getting trapped in his own words, for Jephthah was insecure. The spirit of the Lord had stirred him, yet he was not sure of God's presence. Rather than trusting, he seems to try harder to please God, to act the part of the man of faith and cement the relationship with something definite. It might have been more faithful if he had simply got on with the task in hand and let the Spirit be responsible for the results.

Jephthah won the battle and, in winning, blighted himself and his home. He had not known where his vow would lead. It was just a careless offering of a life—some life or other—that was not his to give. His homecoming sees laughter fall into silence, as father and daughter come face to face in confusion and tears.

You will need to make your own response to this story—particularly if you have not come across it before. You may feel as if this incident comes from another world and has no point of contact with ours. You may want to howl in protest that anyone could offer God such an awful promise. You may think of the people who depend on you and our responsibility to care for one another. You may recall the damage still done by foolish words and the casual ways in which our world can deal with human life. The Bible does not commend Jephthah's vow.

Sunday reflection

'Set a guard over my mouth, O Lord; keep watch over the door of my lips' (Psalm 141:3).

JP

Judges 11:35–40 (NRSV, abridged)

Weeping for the future

When he saw her, he tore his clothes, and said, 'Alas, my daughter! … I have opened my mouth to the Lord, and I cannot take back my vow.' She said to him, 'My father, if you have opened your mouth to the Lord, do to me according to what has gone out of your mouth…' And she said… '… Grant me two months, so that I may go and wander on the mountains, and bewail my virginity, my companions and I.' … At the end of two months, she returned to her father, who did with her according to the vow he had made… So there arose an Israelite custom that for four days every year the daughters of Israel would go out to lament the daughter of Jephthah.

This dreadful incident is far from our present world of human rights and child protection. A young life is taken and no one speaks to stop it. Jephthah, of course, is carrying through his awful vow and some writers on Judges see a very deep kind of faithfulness in that, but the greater dignity surely belongs to the girl.

She appears as a teenager, on the threshold of adult life, not quite ready for marriage but old enough to be aware of this. Her attitude to her father's vow is submissive, though with steadfastness in it, too. She makes herself part of the vow's fulfilment—an actor as well as a victim—but first she claims the right to grieve for what it costs, which is maturity, marriage, motherhood.

Judges has been called a book of weeping. It begins and ends in grief (2:4; 21:2). Here the young women's tears invite us to mourn not just the waste of a life, but also the distress into which the whole story of Judges gradually falls. Yet, amid the tears, there are hints of the gospel ahead. Jephthah's unnamed daughter leads our thoughts on to Gethsemane, where Jesus was obedient to his father's will (Mark 14:32–42). Like him she goes to her death, innocent and aware, from among a company of friends. As friends gather to meet in her memory, her faithful commitment is a mark of sorrow and love for the generations to come.

Reflection

Remember people who have shown you something of Christ amid circumstances of great stress and sorrow.

JP

The gift of the Bible

I love the Bible. It's a treasure trove of compelling stories, practical sense, deep wisdom, spiritual insight and passionate prayer.

I love writing about the Bible, too. I find it fascinating to read the insights of scholars who have studied its history, its structure and its language. I've been a Christian for 35 years, but no matter how many times I read even the most familiar passage, there always seems to be new meaning and guidance to be gained.

So, it upsets me when I hear the Bible being abused—used to maintain power over others, justify inequality, in a way that I believe contradicts its main themes of justice, peace, love and community. It upsets me, too, when people interpret the Bible in ways that I think are directly contrary to the values of Jesus.

The Bible speaks of itself using many images, including a lamp, voice, path, sword. It talks of its words being as sweet as honey, but also as a raging fire or bitter taste. These images seem to express the double-edged nature of the Bible: it reassures and challenges, rebukes and encourages. If C.S. Lewis' Aslan is 'not a tame lion', this is not a tame book! Sometimes it reminds me of *The Monster Book of Monsters* on Harry Potter's reading list—a book that has to be bound with a leather belt to stop it biting.

I fear that at times we have done exactly that with the Bible—that is, tied it up and tamed it so that people actually believe it is about religion rather than human life and its meaning. It is not a collection of holy regulations, but, rather, a book full of comedy, tragedy and even sex and violence. If it were published today for the first time, the Church might want to ban it!

In these notes I have explored various aspects of how I think the Bible is best interpreted and how it 'works' in our lives. The Bible itself gives us a lot of guidance on how to read and understand it. The bottom line is that it is all about Jesus. It builds up to him, reveals him, shows us his significance, brings us into relationship with him and shows us how to live like him. If you read it with him in mind, you can't go too far wrong.

Veronica Zundel

A master key

Long ago God spoke to our ancestors in many and various ways by the prophets, but in these last days he has spoken to us by a Son, whom he appointed heir of all things, through whom he also created the worlds. He is the reflection of God's glory and the exact imprint of God's very being, and he sustains all things by his powerful word.

Hans Denck, a 16th-century Anabaptist, wrote, 'I value Scripture above all things, but not so highly as the Word of God'. What on earth was he getting at?

In everyday talk, we may refer to the Bible as 'the word of God', but actually this is not really accurate. Jesus, as the Bible itself tells us, is the living Word, of which the Bible is only a record. As we read at the beginning of John's Gospel, 'In the beginning was the Word, and the Word was with God, and the Word was God' (John 1:1). We need to remember this when we get all het up about our differing interpretations of scripture. Of course it is essential to work out how God wants us to live, but if we do not debate the issues in the peacemaking spirit of Christ, we are already disobeying God.

Our reading today from the beginning of Hebrews is my personal charter for interpreting the Bible—what scholars call a 'hermeneutical key' (hermeneutics is the science of interpretation).

I believe that God gradually revealed truths about God and the world to the Jewish people, according to what they were capable of understanding. They wrote down what God revealed, not by a kind of 'automatic writing', but using the language and imagery of their own day.

We should always remember, though, that the greatest revelation of God's nature was when God appeared as a human being, living a human life, so we can no longer approach any scripture independently of that life—it is our key to unlocking this ancient collection of books. The whole Bible must be read in the light of Jesus, the Word of God. It is his Spirit who will lead us into all truth.

Reflection

'Then beginning with Moses and all the prophets, he interpreted to them the things about himself in all the scriptures' (Luke 24:27).

VZ

More than useful

But as for you, continue in what you have learned and firmly believed, knowing from whom you learned it, and how from childhood you have known the sacred writings that are able to instruct you for salvation through faith in Christ Jesus. All scripture is inspired by God and is useful for teaching, for reproof, for correction, and for training in righteousness, so that everyone who belongs to God may be proficient, equipped for every good work.

The Bible makes some mind-blowing claims about Jesus. He is 'the image of the invisible God, the firstborn of all creation… He himself is before all things, and in him all things hold together' (Colossians 1:15, 17). In contrast to this, the claims the Bible makes for itself appear quite humble: it is, like the slave Onesimus (Philemon 11), 'useful'.

Is that all? Is the Bible just a useful tool in the Christian's toolbox, like a wrench or a spanner (admittedly an infinitely adjustable one, given how we often 'use' it!)? Many people prefer to think of it instead as the instruction manual for life—maybe like one of those health books in which you can look up any ailment.

Personally, I think that even to regard the Bible as a sort of 'handy home book of everything', an encyclopedia of the good life, is to short-change it. Look more closely at what Paul says to Timothy. What does it mean to be 'instructed for salvation'? In the Bible's own view, salvation is much more than a ticket to heaven: it is the total re-creation of both ourselves and the world we live in, so that we and it reflect God's loving values.

While we are waiting for this new creation, the Bible is able to teach, reprove, correct and train us in righteousness (v. 16). I don't even know a person who manages to do all those things, yet here Paul is claiming that a book can. That has to be a very special book and one that is not so much an instruction manual as a book of miraculous transformation. No wonder Paul calls it 'the sacred writings' and 'God-breathed' (the literal translation of 'inspired by God'). We'd better read it carefully, then!

Prayer

'Open my eyes, so that I may behold wondrous things out of your law'
(Psalm 119:18).

VZ

Words of fire

O Lord, you have enticed me, and I was enticed; you have over-powered me, and you have prevailed. I have become a laughing stock all day long; everyone mocks me. For whenever I speak, I must cry out, I must shout, 'Violence and destruction!' For the word of the Lord has become for me a reproach and derision all day long. If I say, 'I will not mention him, or speak any more in his name,' then within me there is something like a burning fire shut up in my bones; I am weary with holding it in, and I cannot.

An ancient Chinese poem describes the poet waking up in the night, lighting a lamp and quickly writing down a poem before he forgets it, while his wife looks on, thinking he's mad. I must admit that when I am inspired in the night, I often go back to sleep. Next morning, of course, the poem is completely gone!

The words that the prophet Jeremiah here feels compelled to speak are not so easily forgotten. They are a fire in his bones; they burst out of him against his will. Perhaps this is a better image for how the Bible is inspired than the one of a scribe sitting down and taking God's dictation.

The words of the Bible arise out of passion—a passion for God, the passion of God. This book, or rather this library of books, is a record of things that just had to be said. When we read the Bible in church, we often use a solemn, fairly flat voice. Some Christian tra-ditions even recommend this, so that the humanity of the reader will not get in the way of the mes-sage. However, human and divine emotions are what the Bible is all about. When we open it, fire should spring out of its pages and enter our blood. As you prepare to read 'the lesson' in church, feel the fire in it, so that you can convey it to your hearers.

Reflection

'I was silent and still; I held my peace to no avail; my distress grew worse, my heart became hot within me. While I mused, the fire burned; then I spoke with my tongue' (Psalm 39:2–3). What might God be asking you to speak out about?

VZ

From speech to writing

In the fourth year of King Jehoiakim son of Josiah of Judah, this word came to Jeremiah from the Lord: 'Take a scroll and write on it all the words that I have spoken to you against Israel and Judah and all the nations, from the day I spoke to you, from the days of Josiah until today. It may be that when the house of Judah hears of all the disasters that I intend to do to them, all of them may turn from their evil ways, so that I may forgive their iniquity and their sin.' Then Jeremiah called Baruch son of Neriah, and Baruch wrote on a scroll at Jeremiah's dictation all the words of the Lord that he had spoken to him. And Jeremiah ordered Baruch, saying, 'I am prevented from entering the house of the Lord; so you go yourself, and on a fast day in the hearing of the people in the Lord's house you shall read the words of the Lord from the scroll that you have written at my dictation.'

Before the written Bible we have now came into being, there was a long oral tradition—prophecies, sayings, stories and laws memorized by dedicated people. On this side of the written record stands a long line of translators who made that literature available to us. Today we commemorate Jerome, a fourth-century scholar who spent at least four years in the desert teaching himself Hebrew. Then, with the Greek he already knew, he was able to translate both the Old and New Testaments into Latin, which was the common European language of the time.

If you can do so, reading the Bible in its original languages can be very illuminating. However, from the earliest days of the Church, its leaders wanted to make the Bible's treasures available to as many different groups of people as possible and in their own words and idioms. The same wish motivates Bible translators today.

As an occasional translator myself (from German), I know how hard it can be to find just the right equivalent word or phrase. Let's be grateful for those like Jerome who laboured to give us God's wisdom.

Reflection

'Many of the Jews read this inscription, because the place where Jesus was crucified was near the city; and it was written in Hebrew, in Latin, and in Greek' (John 19:20).

VZ

Not easily silenced

Then all the officials sent Jehudi... to say to Baruch, 'Bring the scroll that you read in the hearing of the people, and come.' So Baruch son of Neriah took the scroll in his hand and came to them... When they heard all the words, they turned to one another in alarm, and said to Baruch, 'We certainly must report all these words to the king.' ... Now the king was sitting in his winter apartment (it was the ninth month), and there was a fire burning in the brazier before him. As Jehudi read three or four columns, the king would cut them off with a penknife and throw them into the fire in the brazier, until the entire scroll was consumed... Now, after the king had burned the scroll with the words that Baruch wrote at Jeremiah's dictation, the word of the Lord came to Jeremiah: 'Take another scroll and write on it all the former words that were in the first scroll, which King Jehoiakim of Judah has burned.'

Imagine that you spent weeks writing a report for work and then, before you'd backed the document up on your computer, you accidentally hit the wrong key and deleted the whole lot. Aaargh!

How would Jeremiah feel when Baruch brought him the news of the king's drastic editing methods? Worse than that, I'm sure, but he simply went back to work and dictated all his prophecies to Baruch again—which is why we now have them.

What this story says to me is that there is something enduring about the Bible. These age-old stories, from a culture different in so many ways from ours, somehow still echo across the centuries and shed new light on our daily living for God's kingdom. Even under regimes where possession of a Bible is a criminal offence, God hasn't been silenced. People smuggled in Bibles; people memorized as much of the Bible as they could. It reminds me of Jesus asking the disciples, 'Do you also wish to go away?' and Simon Peter's reply, 'Lord, to whom can we go? You have the words of eternal life' (John 6:67–68).

Prayer

Pray for all for whom the Bible has become a burden instead of a blessing. Pray that they will find new life in its stories.

VZ

Call the first witness

Since many have undertaken to set down an orderly account of the events that have been fulfilled among us, just as they were handed on to us by those who from the beginning were eyewitnesses and servants of the word, I too decided, after investigating everything carefully from the very first, to write an orderly account for you, most excellent Theophilus, so that you may know the truth concerning the things about which you have been instructed.

It was a frosty January morning and I was driving downhill. Suddenly a car came out from a side road on my left and cut right in front of me. I braked with all my might, but still went straight into the other car, doing considerable damage to my new car but very little to the other driver's.

Shakily, we exchanged addresses and insurance details. I was wondering how I'd get home as I had no money with me and the car (let alone myself) was unfit to drive. Suddenly, from around the corner came another parent from my son's school, where I had just dropped him off. Not only did she offer me a lift, but she had also seen the whole thing. I had a witness.

Luke's testimony, and that of the other New Testament writers, is not like someone who happened to see a car crash and might get the details wrong. It is more like someone who has studied for three years with a famous teacher and can now recite all their favourite sayings. Suppose, if my car incident had gone to court, that my witness described my car as silver when it was actually gold. That wouldn't affect the central truth, which was that the accident was not my fault.

Similarly, there are some minor contradictions in the Bible and some stories that have gone through many centuries of retelling and reshaping. God chose to convey truth through fallible human beings. It is also true, however, that these writings have been put together with great care and thought, by God-inspired people who wanted to convey truths about God and life. Some of the facts may be difficult to establish, but truth is not just a matter of facts.

Sunday reflection
What kind of truth are you encountering at church this morning?

VZ

Sweet somethings

The law of the Lord is perfect, reviving the soul; the decrees of the Lord are sure, making wise the simple; the precepts of the Lord are right, rejoicing the heart; the commandment of the Lord is clear, enlightening the eyes; the fear of the Lord is pure, enduring forever; the ordinances of the Lord are true and righteous altogether. More to be desired are they than gold, even much fine gold; sweeter also than honey, and drippings of the honeycomb. Moreover by them is your servant warned; in keeping them there is great reward.

Are you one of those people who can always quote the Bible, chapter and verse, for any eventuality of life? I'm not. I'm more of an 'It's in Luke somewhere… or it might be in John or is it one of the epistles?' sort of person.

No matter how well you know your way from Adam to Zion, though, you only really know the Bible when you attempt to live it. Then, experience takes over from theory and, at that point, I suspect, we are all equally beginners.

In Juan Carlos Ortiz' book *Disciple*, he describes a novel way of approaching Bible study. A discipleship group would read perhaps one verse together and discuss it. Then they would go their separate ways and try to practise it in their lives. The next week they would meet, read the same passage and discuss together how well they'd got on with doing it. They would stay in exactly the same place in the Bible until they all felt that they had begun to get to grips with this particular teaching. Only then would they read something new.

It doesn't work with all of scripture, of course, as not all of it is direct teaching. However, it's a striking way of doing what James tells us: 'But be doers of the word, and not merely hearers who deceive themselves. For if any are hearers of the word and not doers, they are like those who look at themselves in a mirror; for they look at themselves and, on going away, immediately forget what they were like' (James 1:22–24).

Reflection

God's message is like gold and honey: beautiful and delicious. Do we sometimes make it like granite and lemon: hard and bitter?

VZ

A lucky day

When he [Jesus] came to Nazareth, where he had been brought up, he went to the synagogue on the Sabbath day, as was his custom. He stood up to read, and the scroll of the prophet Isaiah was given to him. He unrolled the scroll and found the place where it was written: 'The Spirit of the Lord is upon me, because he has anointed me to bring good news to the poor. He has sent me to proclaim release to the captives and recovery of sight to the blind, to let the oppressed go free, to proclaim the year of the Lord's favour.' And he rolled up the scroll, gave it back to the attendant, and sat down.

Just how lucky must Jesus have felt when they gave him the scroll of Isaiah to read from? Each scroll only holds a single Bible book, so the chances of this one being chosen were only 1 in 39. Alternatively, did Jesus perhaps choose to visit this particular synagogue on a day when he knew that they would be reading Isaiah?

Either way, what an amazing occasion to be present at: the day when the eternal Word, God's ultimate self-expression, reads and preaches from the written word of Hebrew scriptures. Even more, to be there when he preaches from Isaiah—the book that contains those marvellous 'servant songs', which later generations would interpret as prophesying the coming of Jesus among us 'as one who serves' (Luke 22:27).

Yet, Jesus chooses not to speak on one of these subjects, but on Isaiah's 'social charter' (Isaiah 61).

Here, at the beginning of his ministry, he declares his priorities: the poor, imprisoned, disabled, oppressed. He also announces a jubilee year: the year when slaves were freed and all land returned to the clans who originally owned it; a year of economic redistribution and justice.

What is his comment on this passage? It is, 'Today this scripture has been fulfilled in your hearing' (v. 21). In other words, 'This is all about me'. If you hear the Bible being used to justify inequality or oppression or in any way that marginalizes the agenda of Jesus, be suspicious.

Reflection

We are even luckier than the Nazarenes who heard this sermon, as we have the power and opportunity to put it into practice worldwide.

VZ

Unpopular interpretation

And he [Jesus] said, 'Truly I tell you, no prophet is accepted in the prophet's home town. But the truth is, there were many widows in Israel in the time of Elijah, when the heaven was shut up three years and six months, and there was a severe famine over all the land; yet Elijah was sent to none of them except to a widow at Zarephath in Sidon. There were also many lepers in Israel in the time of the prophet Elisha, and none of them was cleansed except Naaman the Syrian.'

In an online discussion forum the other night, I was discussing whether a church should ever ban an individual from preaching. Some thought all opinions should be heard and discussed; others felt that preaching should be restricted to those who agreed with that church's entire basis of faith.

If those at the synagogue in Nazareth had had such a discussion, I think that they would have opted for banning Jesus (and, indeed, that's just what they did, without any discussion, vv. 28–29). His use of scripture is provocative to say the least. First of all, he is not preaching from the passage he read, but, instead, responding to remarks from the congregation. Second, he is more or less saying that God habitually chooses individuals from outside the chosen people to do God's work. No wonder they wanted to kill him!

Jesus' use of the Old Testament, which is frequent, is always bold, creative and thought-provoking—as is the use the Gospel writers and apostles make of scripture. We never hear any tired and worn 'standard' interpretations from them.

The first time I ever preached, it was to a congregation of 450 in a famous charismatic church. Afterwards, I heard an elderly lady say, 'This church is going from bad to worse'. I was consoled by the fact that Jesus' preaching, too, was disliked. I was also heartened by an encounter over coffee with someone who felt excluded by the church, but had felt, for the first time, included by my sermon. My preaching may have been a bit inflammatory, but I think I'd got my priorities right: to focus on the needy, the afraid, those who need comfort most.

Prayer

Lord, teach those of us who preach to disturb the comfortable and comfort the disturbed.

VZ

Under your skin

The days are surely coming, says the Lord, when I will make a new covenant with the house of Israel and the house of Judah. It will not be like the covenant that I made with their ancestors when I took them by the hand to bring them out of the land of Egypt—a covenant that they broke, though I was their husband, says the Lord. But this is the covenant that I will make with the house of Israel after those days, says the Lord: I will put my law within them, and I will write it on their hearts; and I will be their God, and they shall be my people.

Queen Mary Tudor famously said, 'When I am dead and opened, you shall find "Calais" lying in my heart'. So, if you ever need to find Calais…

Bad jokes aside, what might an autopsy find written on our hearts? The metaphorical 'writing' that we leave behind us is made up of our deeds and attitudes—and they are made up of what God (or the world) has first written on us.

Jeremiah promises here that, one day, God's values—the love of God and neighbour—will not just be written in a book, but engraved in our spirit. From a visit to Israel, I brought back a drawing of Ruth sitting in a cornfield clutching her gleanings. The whole of Ruth's body in the picture is made up of the book of Ruth, in Hebrew, written in a spiral. I like that as an image of how God's Law—the priorities and wisdom of God—can seep into us so much that they are in our very bones and bloodstream.

Today, we honour William Tyndale—the most influential English Bible translator, whose turn of phrase is still very evident in the King James Version of the Bible. He translated the Bible into the common tongue of his day, but his 16th-century English is now a foreign language to us. For the Bible to sink deep into our system, we need first to hear or read it in words that we can understand.

Reflection

When the whole of the Bible's wisdom is written into our very flesh, we will not need Bibles any more. However, I doubt that it will be this side of the resurrection!

VZ

Judges 12—16

The book of Judges tells of an ancient, wild time in the history of the people of Israel. It is set before 1000BC, before the kings and the temple, and describes a people who are not fully settled in the Promised Land. They are just gaining control of parts of it from various foreign tribes. Sometimes they have the upper hand; sometimes they don't. God raises up judges—that is, rulers who lead the people for a generation, but whose influence doesn't last. It's all part of the story of Israel obeying God and flourishing, then wandering away and suffering for it—like the cycles of our own lives.

Many of the judges are unconventional characters, subversive even. There is Deborah, a woman; Ehud, who is left-handed; and Samson, an untamed strongman. Many of their stories are like folk tales, focusing on feats of heroism, trickery and slaughter against more settled enemies.

The origins of the book of Judges are obscure. It was probably composed in about the seventh century BC, possibly under the reforming King Josiah. It is usually seen as part of a literature that views nationalistic and religious struggles as bound together. There are no qualms about killing the enemies of the people as they are God's enemies, too. The aim of the book was to inspire the Israelites.

Samson typifies this. His victories are celebrated as sacred triumphs, without any worries about the casualties. As a folk hero with amazing powers, he has been compared to other characters in legends both ancient and modern—from Hercules to Superman. However, he is a holy hero, dedicated to the Lord before birth, his strength coming directly from God. In him, physical prowess and holiness are united, the one springing from the other.

Samson's story is a wonderful, rich tale that has inspired poets, artists and filmmakers, from John Milton to Cecil B. DeMille. Perhaps, though, the story is less popular now than it once was. It is not in my five-year-old son's children's Bible, whereas I remember it from Sunday school. This might be due to embarrassment about sex and violence—two of the most important forces in the world. Surely, though, we have to grapple with such subjects head on rather than retreat into our alternatives of self-serving cosiness and self-destructive bickering. We can be in the world without being of it.

Rachel Boulding

Friday 7 October

JUDGES 12:5–6 (NRSV)

Who is in and who is out

Then the Gileadites took the fords of the Jordan against the Ephraimites. Whenever one of the fugitives of Ephraim said, 'Let me go over', the men of Gilead would say to him, 'Are you an Ephraimite?' When he said, 'No', they said to him, 'Then say Shibboleth', and he said, 'Sibboleth', for he could not pronounce it right. Then they seized him and killed him at the fords of the Jordan. Forty-two thousand of the Ephraimites fell at that time.

Our chapters begin with the end of Jephthah's six-year rule as judge of Israel. Jephthah's life has begun unpromisingly (see Judges 11): he was the son of a prostitute, whose half-brothers drove him away. Later, he made a vow to offer as a sacrifice to God the first person who greeted him after battle—inevitably, it was his only child. The end of the chapter relates chillingly that he 'did with her according to the vow he had made' (11:39).

As so often in the Old Testament, no comment is made about whether or not this is a good idea. Our passage shows a similar lack of passion, as it records the slaughter of 42,000 Ephraimites who were fighting against the Gileadites (who included Jephthah). The Gileadites have a test for Ephraimite deserters —they have to pronounce the word 'Shibboleth'. Thus, 'Shibboleth' has come to mean a test of belonging to a tribe, like a badge identifying a group.

Of course, we can easily find such tests now, especially in the Church. For instance, there is the jargon we use, an obvious example of which is the terms for the Communion service, the various theological stances and groups having their own words for it. So much of this is about wanting to belong, but in a way that defines who is in and who is out. Often, this desire for identity is connected to an honest desire for purity, but one that becomes distorted. Wanting to see ourselves in a special group and be 'clean' has become a need to see external 'purity' in others before they can join—partly because of fear of the unfamiliar or accusations of sins that happen not to tempt us. We need to examine our motives carefully before regarding other sinners as further beyond the pale than us.

Reflection

'What God has made clean, you must not call profane' (Acts 10:15).

RB

47

Dedicated to holiness

And the angel of the Lord appeared to the woman [Manoah's wife] and said to her, 'Although you are barren, having borne no children, you shall conceive and bear a son. Now be careful not to drink wine or strong drink, or to eat anything unclean, for you shall conceive and bear a son. No razor is to come on his head, for the boy shall be a Nazirite to God from birth. It is he who shall begin to deliver Israel from the hand of the Philistines.'

Now we reach the meat of these chapters—the story of Samson. It begins with a familiar scenario: a previously barren woman gives birth to a son, who is to be dedicated to the Lord. The clearest comparisons are with Hannah (1 Samuel 1) and Elizabeth (Luke 1:5–25, 57–80), though there are also similarities with Sarah, Rebecca and Rachel in the book of Genesis. Each birth is miraculous, coming after years of the misery of unwanted childlessness. All the parents in these three stories—Hannah and Elkanah, Elizabeth and Zechariah, as well as Manoah and his wife—are keen to offer their children back to God as they know a blessing when they see one.

The idea of being a Nazirite is described in Numbers 6:1–21, where God tells Moses that men and women can make a vow to dedicate themselves to the Lord and separate themselves from strong drink and cutting their hair. The word 'Nazirite' means both dedication and separation. It's usually a form of holiness that individuals choose for a particular time. Samson is unusual in being declared to be one even before he is born.

It's not a contradiction to praise the dedication of a Nazirite while questioning the unhealthy extremes to which the quest for this type of purity can lead, as we saw yesterday. Being a Nazirite was meant to be unusual, with few being called to such a demanding response to God. We can all try to be as holy as possible, under God's guidance, without judging others. The parable of the workers in the vineyard is instructive here (Matthew 20:1–16), as are Jesus' words about motes and beams (Luke 6:41–42). We should work out our own salvation and allow others the freedom to do the same.

Prayer

Lord, have mercy on me,
a sinner, too.

RB

Sunday 9 October

JUDGES 13:10–11, 15–18 (NRSV, ABRIDGED)

Too wonderful to be named

So the woman ran quickly and told her husband, 'The man who came to me the other day has appeared to me.' Manoah got up and followed his wife... Manoah said to the angel of the Lord, 'Allow us to detain you, and prepare a kid for you.' The angel of the Lord said to Manoah, 'If you detain me, I will not eat your food; but if you want to prepare a burnt offering, then offer it to the Lord.' (For Manoah did not know that he was the angel of the Lord.) Then Manoah said... 'What is your name, so that we may honour you when your words come true?' But the angel... said to him, 'Why do you ask my name? It is too wonderful.'

Manoah's wife is the focus of much of this chapter, but she is never named. It might seem odd that Manoah asks the angel's name 'so that we may honour you' (v. 17), but whoever set down the story didn't do the same about 'the woman'. The angel's name is 'too wonderful', but it is as if the woman's name is just too lowly to bother with.

Of course, we should be wary of reading our assumptions into a culture that is completely different in time, place and concerns, but some of us cannot help wondering why this key figure isn't dignified with a name. The flow of the story was more important than remembering petty details such as names, however: what mattered more was the way that God provided a miraculous son. It's more vital to establish that God is at work and that the boy will become a special man.

Manoah and his wife don't need the details to give thanks. They trust and believe immediately and work together to make sure that they both hear the message clearly about their son after the angel has appeared to the woman alone. They are eager to listen to and then to honour the angel. Unlike Job, they don't seem to need reminding of God's grandeur: their response is one of immediate respect and gratitude. When God blesses us, do we react like this or do we somehow expect good times to flow, as if we deserved them?

Sunday reflection

Father, help me to carry my Sunday thanksgiving into the whole week.

RB

The Twentieth Sunday after Trinity 49

JUDGES 13:19–23 (NRSV, ABRIDGED)

God calls a capable woman

So Manoah… offered it [the kid]… to the Lord, to him who works wonders. When the flame went up towards heaven from the altar, the angel of the Lord ascended in the flame… Then Manoah realized that it was the angel of the Lord. And Manoah said to his wife, 'We shall surely die, for we have seen God.' But his wife said to him, 'If the Lord had meant to kill us, he would not have accepted a burnt offering and a grain offering at our hands, or shown us all these things, or now announced to us such things as these.'

Here Manoah and his wife realize the true character of the messenger who they have met. They must have sensed that he was holy as he spoke a prophecy about a son whose birth no ordinary person would have foreseen, but when the messenger ascends from their offering, they know he is an angel.

Manoah panics and seems to confuse God with his angel. His wife, showing the tact that many women have to display around the times of their husbands' wilder outbursts, is more logical. She intelligently works out three reasons for it being unlikely that God means to kill them. It looks as if, yet again, God is using the good sense of a woman to bring his purposes about. Despite her insignificance in the world's eyes, this woman's native wit is so valuable that it can be used in God's plans.

This feels like an example of God deploying what the world despises in order to show that there is a more excellent way. He calls on women, such as Hannah, Elizabeth and Mary, and, later at his resurrection, Mary Magdalene, to serve him using their distinctive talents—things that powerful men just don't have to offer. It would have been easy for all these women to make excuses and question what impact they could ever have from the bottom of such a male-dominated hierarchy. We've got even less excuse now, when at least some of the constraints of gender, as well as class and ethnic background, have been swept aside. We've all got talents that God can use—not only cooking and cleaning, but befriending, organizing and much else besides.

Prayer

Lord and Father of us all, show us how we can serve you.

RB

JUDGES 14:2–9 (NRSV, ABRIDGED)

His wonders to perform

Then he [Samson] came up, and told his father and mother, 'I saw a Philistine woman at Timnah; now get her for me as my wife.' But his father and mother said to him, 'Is there not a woman among your kin...?' ... His father and mother did not know that this was from the Lord; for he was seeking a pretext to act against the Philistines... When he [Samson] came to the vineyards of Timnah, suddenly a young lion roared at him. The spirit of the Lord rushed on him, and he tore the lion apart with his bare hands as one might tear apart a kid... After a while... he turned aside to see the carcase of the lion, and there was a swarm of bees in the body of the lion, and honey. He scraped it out into his hands, and went on, eating as he went.

The Lord's ways seem particularly mysterious here. Samson's parents reluctantly cave in, not knowing that his marriage to a Philistine is part of a larger plan. Samson is clearly blessed, as we see from his encounter with the lion, and he is given his superhuman strength direct from God. This leads to the mysterious episode with the honey. Samson takes the sweetness on offer and goes on his way.

In both his unexpected choice of wife and the vividly detailed victory against the lion, there is a sense of anticipation, of being on the verge of greater events. It's a bit like when I'm reading a story with my son and he asks, all the time, 'Why did he do that?' Of course, I answer, 'Let's carry on reading and find out.'

We have to be content to wait and ponder the puzzles in our hearts (like Mary after Jesus had gone missing in the temple in Luke 2:51), but not give up or assume that we're being led towards a dead end. We can't expect wonderful experiences to fall into our laps, as if the world owes us a living. Even positive events, such as friendships, marriage, children and worthwhile work, don't come neatly labelled with meanings. We can enjoy them as gifts, thanking God for them and trusting him for his overall purpose.

Reflection

Our meddling intellect
Misshapes the beauteous
forms of things:
We murder to dissect.

William Wordsworth (1770–1850)

RB

JUDGES 14:12–14 (NRSV, ABRIDGED)

Out of strength comes sweetness

Samson said to them [his wedding guests], 'Let me now put a riddle to you. If you can explain it to me within the seven days of the feast, and find it out, then I will give you thirty linen garments and thirty festal garments. But if you cannot explain it to me, then you shall give me thirty linen garments and thirty festal garments.' … He said to them, 'Out of the eater came something to eat. Out of the strong came something sweet.'

Samson lays down the challenge of his riddle of the honey from the lion's body. Whichever of the two parties loses has to provide expensive garments (enough to 'impoverish', v. 15). Suddenly the feast has turned ugly.

It's like those moments towards the end of Shakespeare's *Twelfth Night*, when the jokes turn sour. The puritan Malvolio, whose smugness has been a pain throughout the play, deserves a good kicking (at least metaphorically), but not to the extent of what the 'jokers' do, throwing him into a dark, friendless prison. The tricksters have crossed the line and the play's atmosphere hovers uncomfortably between farce and tragedy.

It looks as if Samson was searching for an excuse to strike back at the Philistines who had ruled his country for a generation. While he has some cause—the Philistines seem to have been ruthless oppressors—tricking them with riddles is hardly an effective way to resolve the situation, although riddling competitions were part of weddings in many traditional societies.

No wonder the guests are stumped. The combination 'Out of strength comes forth sweetness' is intriguing, mingling fear and power with softness and tastiness. You can see why it's striking enough to be used, unchanged, for many decades on the logo for Lyle's Golden Syrup.

Strength and sweetness offer a rich interplay. They can point to God and his blessings. We can think of the lion's power—more often seen in a menacing prowl than actual combat. It's the latent ability that impresses. It's not surprising that C.S. Lewis depicted his benign figure of authority, Aslan, as a lion. Then the sweetness hints at God's gifts to us: 'O taste and see that the Lord is good' (Psalm 34:8).

Reflection

Ponder on the effect of strength and sweetness in your life.

RB

JUDGES 14:16–20 (NRSV, ABRIDGED)

Betrayal and murder

So Samson's wife wept before him, saying, 'You hate me; you do not really love me. You have asked a riddle of my people, but you have not explained it to me.'... She wept before him for the seven days that their feast lasted; and because she nagged him, on the seventh day he told her. Then she explained the riddle to her people... Then the spirit of the Lord rushed on him, and he went down to Ashkelon. He killed thirty men of the town, took their spoil, and gave the festal garments to those who had explained the riddle. In hot anger he went back to his father's house. And Samson's wife was given to his companion, who had been his best man.

Here we have Samson's most vulnerable characteristic, which is his inability to stand his ground with women. Here and later on, they twist him round their little finger and he falls for it every time. Samson's wife (unnamed, like his mother) has been threatened with death by her people (v. 15), so she, too, is under pressure.

Samson, however, is seized by the Lord's spirit into terrible violence. The way the story is told doesn't mention any qualms on Samson's part, just that 'the spirit of the Lord rushed on him' (v. 19). Can we really attribute the killing of 30 otherwise unknown and innocent men to some grand but mysterious plan of God's? I think such questions have to be asked on some levels; we need to be honest in our responses. On other levels, however, such questions misunderstand the nature of the story. We are rightly shocked by the slaughter, despite being caught up in the sweep of the tale as a whole.

Suffering is one of the mysteries that we need to examine again and again, so central is it to both ordinary human life and our faith in Jesus, who died in agony. Pain is one of the main reasons people give for not believing in God and we must never forget that there are no simple answers—otherwise everyone would worship God gladly.

We must keep exploring our good news and present it afresh in every generation, not being afraid to admit that we don't understand it all perfectly.

Reflection

'By his wounds we are healed'
(Isaiah 53:5, NIV).

RB

Hitting back after hurt

Samson went to visit his wife, bringing along a kid… But her father would not allow him to go in. Her father said, 'I was sure that you had rejected her; so I gave her to your companion…' Samson said to them, 'This time, when I do mischief to the Philistines, I will be without blame.' So Samson went and caught 300 foxes, and took some torches; and he turned the foxes tail to tail, and put a torch between each pair of tails. When he had set fire to the torches, he let the foxes go into the standing grain of the Philistines, and burned up the shocks and the standing grain, as well as the vineyards and olive groves.

As we saw yesterday, it can be hard to know how to approach stories like these about Samson, especially when we are looking for help with our faith. This part of Holy Scripture doesn't seem very holy, even if we can say of it, 'Here's an example of what not to do.'

We can, of course, make more of an effort to see what the original audience saw in these sacred texts. When we try to understand what Samson meant to the Israelites— that he was a national saviour, saving them from the Philistines—we might be able to have a deeper sense of what he could mean for us. This might require our setting aside for a while our quite legitimate revulsion at the story's elements of destruction in order to focus on what it might be saying to us.

Samson's anger is understandable, but his actions seem totally disproportionate. Yet, it's not as if we in the modern world have 'grown out of' similar actions. We have only to glance at the news from the Holy Land to see this kind of thing almost daily: children killed, farms and businesses wrecked—on both sides.

Have I never hit back in some way at someone who hurt me? Just because there's no body count after my petty fits of pique doesn't give me an excuse for smugness. I could always try taking a step back to see how absurd this might look from the outside—especially from God's viewpoint.

Prayer

Lord and Father of us all, help me to see my actions as you see them.

RB

Inspired by our ancestors

Then the Philistines asked, 'Who has done this?' And they said, 'Samson, the son-in-law of the Timnite, because he has taken Samson's wife and given her to his companion.' So the Philistines came up, and burned her and her father. Samson said to them, 'If this is what you do, I swear I will not stop until I have taken revenge on you.' He struck them down hip and thigh with great slaughter.

Samson has laid waste the Philistines' livelihood, setting in train a tit-for-tat cycle of slaughter and revenge. As we saw yesterday, we can approach all this violence in a number of ways. One is to think of how we can apply such passages to ourselves in a spiritual or metaphorical sense, rather than a literal one. Thus, the foreigners and foes become our own spiritual enemies—our besetting sins and the temptations that we should put to death. There is a long tradition in the Church of interpreting the Bible in this way, so we needn't be wary of it, if it helps us.

Crucially, it doesn't mean that we close our minds to other approaches—something can be both metaphorical and literal. A real event in history can have a symbolic and a deeper significance for us—it doesn't mean that it didn't really happen. This is clearly true of events such as the birth and death of Jesus, but it can also be true of other episodes in the Bible as it can be of any great events or heroic figures from world history. In this way, we can battle against our inner demons, inspired by acts of wartime heroism, whether in the Bible or from conflicts such as World War II.

So often, though, in the story of Samson, as elsewhere in the Old Testament, it is hard to find any straightforward meaning. As we saw in Tuesday's notes, we have to stay with the story, hanging on for the next rollercoaster instalment. Rather than feeling that we need to rush to judgment or interpretation, we can enjoy it unfolding. This is, after all, why the stories have lasted in the popular imagination: they are great tales, with a powerful momentum; gripping page-turners.

Reflection

Think about a historical figure who has inspired you. What do you see in him or her?

RB

Judges 15:14–19 (NRSV, abridged)

Give us this day our daily bread

The spirit of the Lord rushed on him [Samson], and the ropes that were on his arms became like flax that has caught fire, and his bonds melted off his hands. Then he found a fresh jawbone of a donkey, reached down and took it, and with it he killed 1000 men. And Samson said, 'With the jawbone of a donkey, heaps upon heaps, with the jawbone of a donkey I have slain 1000 men.' … By then he was very thirsty, and he called on the Lord, saying, 'You have granted this great victory by the hand of your servant. Am I now to die of thirst, and fall into the hands of the uncircumcised?' So God split open the hollow place that is at Lehi, and water came from it.

Before these verses, Samson has been betrayed by his own people and handed over—bound with ropes—to the Philistines (vv. 9–13). The episode is so memorable partly because of two details that make it easier to visualize. First, the ropes melt away like burning flax and then Samson uses the donkey's jawbone to kill 1000 men. These make it a great tale, as does the satisfying sense of reversal as the bound prisoner triumphs. Yet, the more telling part for us as Christians is what follows: God's approval, shown in the provision of water for the victorious warrior. Like Elijah and Moses, he is fed directly by God.

As we've noted, the violence seems shocking, but the book is one of nationalistic history. Samson is his people's saviour, so the early audiences were looking for a high body count to make it all the more impressive. It's a bit like an old war film: you expect the enemy to die horribly and the brave British (or Americans or Australians or whoever is the target audience) to be blessed with victory.

Samson is in no doubt that his victory comes from the Lord. He turns to God and is rewarded. It's straightforward, but how often do we either attribute any success to God or even simply ask him for daily needs? It ought to be every day, as we're taught from earliest childhood.

Sunday reflection

When you send forth your spirit, we are created; and you renew the face of the earth
(Psalm 104:30, adapted).

RB

This time, he gets away with it

And he [Samson] judged Israel in the days of the Philistines for twenty years. Once Samson went to Gaza, where he saw a prostitute and went in to her. The Gazites were told, 'Samson has come here.' So they encircled the place and lay in wait for him all night at the city gate… thinking, 'Let us wait until the light of the morning; then we will kill him.' But Samson lay only until midnight. Then at midnight he rose up, took hold of the doors of the city gate and the two posts, pulled them up, bar and all, put them on his shoulders, and carried them to the top of the hill.

The first verse above gives the game away, that 20 years fly past in a single sentence—uneventful, unworthy of comment. Some things must have happened, especially in such a powerful position.

At first, this story seems to be yet another example of Samson's strength, as we see him ripping out the city gates to escape, but there are two other key elements. First, his weakness for women. His sexual appetite has led him into a risky situation here, as it did earlier when he married and as it will do again with Delilah. Here, he manages to get away; later on, he will not.

This leads to the second vital element: his intelligence or, if you prefer, his low cunning. He is wise enough not to lie around for too long. Such cleverness is one of the aspects of his character that, presumably, has enabled him to be a judge in Israel for so long, during those 20 years of routine that we hear so little about.

So, this little tale gives a summary of his strengths and weaknesses and tells of a last success before the horrors to come. It's strange that it should be one of very few incidents chosen to be recorded in his long rule. Doesn't that ring true of our own experience, however? Years can fly by, with only a few brief memories to show for them. What can we recall from, say, the year when we were 23? Perhaps only a few visual memories, like snapshots, come to mind. Yet, we can put all our experiences and memories into God's care, trying to see them under the eye of heaven.

Reflection
Lord, for the years, we bring our thanks today.

RB

Enter the femme fatale

After this he fell in love with a woman in the valley of Sorek, whose name was Delilah. The lords of the Philistines came to her and said to her, 'Coax him, and find out what makes his strength so great…' So Delilah said to Samson, 'Please tell me what makes your strength so great…' Samson said to her, 'If they bind me with seven fresh bowstrings that are not dried out, then I shall become weak, and be like anyone else.' Then the lords of the Philistines brought her seven fresh bowstrings… But he snapped the bowstrings… So the secret of his strength was not known.

Here comes Samson's nemesis: his relationship with Delilah. Part of the difficulty with reading this now is that it all seems so obvious. Delilah oozes trouble. She's like a pantomime villain, so much so that I want to shout, 'Behind you!' Can't Samson tell that she's toxic?

Delilah asks Samson about the source of his strength, he gives her a detailed answer and, lo and behold, his answer is immediately tested on him. This should tell Samson all he needs to know about what she is like. This is the point at which the story becomes like a tragedy on stage. The hero has a fatal flaw—his weakness for women—which is his downfall and to which he is blind. Excuse the pun, but it will soon make him blind to everything. We, the audience, can see it, but he can't.

Samson's flaw is like those parts of ourselves or the way we behave that others notice, but we don't. Sometimes these can be merely irritating habits, such as jangling the contents of our pockets or leaving things untidy, but they can be more serious. The only real comfort is that God sees them, whether we can or not. As we noted yesterday, everything falls under his gaze, so he judges without human bias.

Prayer

Lord and sovereign of all the creatures, I humbly present to thy divine majesty, myself, my soul and body, my thoughts and my words, my actions and intentions, my passions and my sufferings, to be disposed by thee to thy glory, to be guided by thy counsel.

Jeremy Taylor (1613–67)

RB

The same old sins again

Then she [Delilah] said to him [Samson], 'How can you say, "I love you", when your heart is not with me? You… have not told me what makes your strength so great.' Finally, after she had nagged him with her words day after day, and pestered him, he was tired to death. So he told her his whole secret, and said to her… '… If my head were shaved, then my strength would leave me…' When Delilah realized that he had told her his whole secret, she sent and called the lords of the Philistines.

Here we see Samson, who ought to know better, finally give way to Delilah's persistence, with the type of tragic inevitability that we found yesterday. Of course, he has been in this position before, with his wife.

I must admit, I bridle at the word 'nagged' (v. 16). In the Authorized Version, it's translated as 'pressed' and 'urged'. Nagging fits with a damaging stereotype of what women do. Often, when they're pushed into a corner and are merely trying to ask for a little fairness—as with a wife whose husband doesn't help much around the house—they are said to be 'nagging'. Usually, it's one of those words that tells you more about the wider situation the woman is in and the lack of cooperation she meets with than what she is actually saying.

Thus, with Delilah, while I wouldn't want to defend her actions, she is using the only power she has to achieve her aims. Similar forms of entrapment have been used by spies for thousands of years to gain knowledge—as they still are today.

Perhaps the behaviour of both Samson and Delilah, in their different ways, isn't so surprising. Neither comes out of it well, but they are familiar types of men and women. At least Delilah has a name, unlike Samson's mother and wife before her. The story has become an archetype, offering a basic pattern for one of the destructive ways in which men and woman can interact. The situation seems corny, but, just because many others have been drawn into sin by sex or the desire for power, this doesn't mean that these temptations are any less dangerous now than they were all those years ago.

Prayer

Father, deliver me from obvious temptations today.

RB

How are the mighty fallen

She [Delilah] let him fall asleep on her lap; and she called a man, and had him shave off the seven locks of his head. He began to weaken… When he awoke from his sleep, he thought, 'I will go out as at other times, and shake myself free.' But he did not know that the Lord had left him. So the Philistines seized him and gouged out his eyes. They brought him down to Gaza and bound him with bronze shackles; and he ground at the mill in the prison… And when their hearts were merry, they said, 'Call Samson, and let him entertain us.'

Here we see Samson at his lowest point. As John Milton (1608–74) famously put it in *Samson Agonistes*, 'Eyeless in Gaza, at the mill with slaves.' Your heart goes out to him—especially as it represents such a reversal in his life as a conqueror and ruler. Milton wrote, 'O dark, dark, dark, amid the blaze of noon, irrecoverably dark, total eclipse without all hope of day!'

The Philistines pile on the agony, tormenting Samson physically and mentally. This offends against our natural sense of justice. A desire to punish the person who has wrecked such devastation on them is natural, but there is something twisted here. The way the Philistines are depicted is surely more than the portrayal of a dastardly enemy nation. It's not just dark malevolence, but a vivid picture of a people without God—bitter, inhuman, delighting in senseless, sadistic torture—and

they don't even seem to realize it. Humiliation of their enemy is all part of a jolly party for them.

This shows how easy it is to slide, gentle stage by gentle stage, into barbarity. The obvious comparison is with Germany in the 1930s, when otherwise decent people were led into the horrors of fascism. Both the Philistines and the Nazis might seem distant to us now, but similar things can happen in apparently civilized countries even today. How is it that we put up with the barbarity of world poverty when we stay rich at the expense of people who lack the basic healthcare and education that we take for granted? We're led into thinking that this offence against God's justice is acceptable.

Prayer

Father, show me your standards; open my eyes to society's blind spots.

RB

Was Samson like a suicide bomber?

Samson said to the attendant who held him by the hand, 'Let me feel the pillars on which the house rests, so that I may lean against them.' Now the house was full of men and women; all the lords of the Philistines were there, and on the roof there were about 3000 men and women, who looked on while Samson performed. Then Samson called to the Lord and said, 'Lord God, remember me and strengthen me only this once, O God, so that with this one act of revenge I may pay back the Philistines for my two eyes... Let me die with the Philistines.'

Samson's triumph in death has always raised questions and has recently become controversial. It's much more than the final revenge on Israel's and Samson's personal enemies. Now some commentators have found in Samson's willingness to die a justification for suicide bombing. If people are sufficiently provoked, won't they react with a desire to make the ultimate sacrifice? Some have seen it as an example of the motivation shared by all who fight for their people—a willingness to die for the cause—but taken to the extreme. It's a different kind of terrorism from those who detonate bombs from a distance.

Perhaps we should explore what seems shocking about calling Samson a terrorist rather than dismiss it out of hand. Is it anything beyond the hackneyed 'One man's terrorist is another man's freedom fighter'? Isn't he more like those in the French Resistance, using vio-lence to free their people from an invader? On the other hand, Samson killed thousands of his enemies, so it could also be said that his revenge is part of the destructive cycle of tit-for-tat violence that is all too familiar today in the Middle East and elsewhere, as we noted last week. Yet, again, many today might say that a truly great man wouldn't want to increase the body count in the way that is celebrated here, that a good man would resist the culture of vengeance and be willing to make concessions, seeking out the good of all. Perhaps we shouldn't strain too much for modern parallels, but focus on the story as it was intended to be received—the cele-bration of a national hero who brought hope to his people.

Reflection

Do you think Samson was a right-eous martyr or a reckless terrorist?

RB

What we can see in a 'death so noble'

[Samson] strained with all his might; and the house fell on the lords and all the people who were in it. So those he killed at his death were more than those he had killed during his life. Then his brothers and all his family came down and took him and brought him up and buried him between Zorah and Eshtaol in the tomb of his father Manoah. He had judged Israel for twenty years.

There's no doubt about the author's attitude to Samson: you can sense the approval in his note of the strong man's final tally of destruction. John Milton shares this sentiment, although the impression that he is protesting too much hints that Samson wasn't seen simply as a hero, even in the seventeenth century: 'Samson hath quit himself like Samson, and heroically hath finish'd a life heroic.'

Inevitably, there is a sense of sadness as a great man dies, especially in such a sacrificial way. As noted earlier, it feels like a tragedy on stage. So, what have we learned from this warrior, both his life of fighting and his 'death so noble' (as Milton put it)?

Part of the value of the story, of course, is that a range of ideas is present at the same time. Fresh ways of seeing it will be found in the future that we can't guess at today—in the same way that differing notions about the position of women, slavery, war and terrorism—which would have been unthinkable to many in the past—can be found now. It shows the strength of the Old Testament that it can stimulate such thinking and still have new things to say.

Can we honour Samson as a straightforward hero? We can hardly hold up his actions as a model for our children—they hear quite enough about sex and violence from our culture as it is. Perhaps we're being overly sophisticated when we raise some of these questions about this figure as a hero. We could celebrate a character who was blessed by the Lord, fought hard for his country, had his share of flaws and suffered bitterly after betrayal, but finally sacrificed himself for his people.

Reflection
God our father, help me to fight like Samson against my inner enemies.

RB

Old Testament kings

The thoughts and desires had been simmering for a long time in the minds of the people of Israel. They wanted to be like all the other nations and have a king to rule over them, someone who would lead them, inspire them, a mighty warrior, a symbol of power and authority. Samuel warned them of the implications of having a king, the price that they would pay, but they had made their minds up and so God said to Samuel, 'Listen to their voice and set a king over them' (1 Samuel 8:22). God chose Saul, Samuel anointed him and presented him to the people. He was eventually succeeded by David, the 'shepherd king' and he in turn by Solomon, renowned for his great wisdom and for building the temple.

Three great but very different kings, their names so familiar. After them came... Who were they? What did they do? During the next two weeks we will be looking at some of them—the good and great, wicked and weak, arrogant and humble, God-fearing and heathen. How did they use or abuse the power that they had? What sort of legacy did they leave behind and what have they to do with us? Can we learn anything from them or are they but shadowy figures whose stories we skip over as we read the Bible, passing on quickly in search of words for today, uninterested in monarchs with strange names from the dim and distant past, whose lives and times bear no resemblance to ours?

We all long for someone to lead us, give us peace, stability, hope and a future. In our 21st century, rulers still rise and fall, promise much, yet achieve little. Are we looking in the wrong direction, demanding more than any human leader can deliver, however promising or powerful? As we look at the Old Testament kings, maybe we will remember that and discover afresh that there is but one true king. It is only as we submit to his rule in our hearts and lives that we will know victory, peace and hope. 'Kings shall bow down before him, and gold and incense bring; all nations shall adore him, his praise all peoples sing: To him shall prayer unceasing and daily vows ascend; his kingdom still increasing, a kingdom without end' (J. Montgomery, 1771–1854).

Margaret Cundiff

1 KINGS 12:3–11, 19 (NRSV, ABRIDGED)

Where was wisdom?

Jeroboam and all the assembly of Israel came and said to Rehoboam, 'Your father made our yoke heavy. Now therefore lighten the hard service of your father and his heavy yoke that he placed on us, and we will serve you.'… Then King Rehoboam took counsel with the older men who had attended his father Solomon while he was still alive, saying, 'How do you advise me to answer this people?' They answered him, 'If you will be a servant to this people… and speak good words to them when you answer them, then they will be your servants for ever.' But he disregarded the advice that the older men gave him, and consulted with the younger men who had grown up with him… The young men… said to him, 'Thus you should say to this people… "My little finger is thicker than my father's loins. Now whereas my father laid on you a heavy yoke, I will add to your yoke…"' … So Israel has been in rebellion against the house of David to this day.

Here was the chance to build a stable kingdom, but Rehoboam threw it away. He listened to, but did not heed, the wise counsel of those who had many years of experience, who knew the way to bring north and south together. Instead, he chose to follow the advice of the young hotheads and so alienated those who had been ready to work in harmony with him. The result was anger, bloodshed, enmity and separation.

It could all have been so different, a united kingdom and people, but the opportunity had been lost because a headstrong man rejected the way of cooperation for that of confrontation and aggression. It is a sorry story, but one still writ large in our world today as the voice of reason seems to go unheeded and continuing oppression and violence plunges us into the depths of sin and suffering.

There is a better way, but it needs people of courage and faith to both proclaim it and live it so that all may enjoy respect and dignity and be able to live in peace and harmony.

Sunday reflection

'What does the Lord require of you, but to do justice, and to love kindness, and to walk humbly with your God?' (Micah 6:8)

MC

A heart that was true

Asa did what was right in the sight of the Lord, as his father David had done. He put away the male temple prostitutes out of the land, and removed all the idols that his ancestors had made. He also removed his mother Maacah from being queen mother, because she had made an abominable image for Asherah; Asa cut down her image and burned it at the Wadi Kidron. But the high places were not taken away. Nevertheless the heart of Asa was true to the Lord all his days. He brought into the house of the Lord the votive gifts of his father, and his own votive gifts—silver, gold, and utensils.

Asa started as he meant to go on. He abolished pagan religion, restored the worship of God and set out to keep God's law and commandments. He not only removed most of the symbols of foreign gods, but also those who had been so much part of the worship of them, including those involved in cult prostitution. He even removed his mother from her position as queen mother because she supported worship of the foreign gods.

Under his rule, Judah had peace and prosperity, it was strong in every way. When the Ethiopians came out against him with a vastly superior army, Asa prayed for God to help him, saying, 'O Lord, you are our God; let no mortal prevail against you' (2 Chronicles 14:11) and God answered his prayer and a great victory was won.

Asa remained an active, zealous, God-fearing king, powerful and secure until the king of Israel rose against him. Asa panicked, made an alliance with the king of Aram and so was saved from defeat, but he had forgotten to call on God for help, choosing human power instead, and when he was confronted with that fact, he acted very cruelly (2 Chronicles 16:10). When he was ill, he did not turn to God either, but to physicians. Did that wipe out the good that he had done? I am sure it did not—he was simply human and human beings sin and make mistakes, even kings! Why not take a look at the whole story (2 Chronicles 14—16 and 1 Kings 15:9–24)? It is a fascinating read and a very challenging one.

Prayer

Lord, help me to trust and serve you in all circumstances.

MC

A force to be reckoned with

In the thirty-eighth year of King Asa of Judah, Ahab son of Omri began to reign over Israel… And as if it had been a light thing for him to walk in the sins of Jeroboam son of Nebat, he took as his wife Jezebel daughter of King Ethbaal of the Sidonians, and went and served Baal, and worshipped him. He erected an altar for Baal in the house of Baal, which he built in Samaria. Ahab also made a sacred pole. Ahab did more to provoke the anger of the Lord, the God of Israel, than had all the kings of Israel who were before him.

Ahab saw the alliance of the Israelites and Canaanites more as political expediency than religious tolerance, but not so his wife. She was determined that her god, Baal, should be the only god, and that all should worship him. She was a powerful influence in directing Ahab's conversion to promoting and serving Baal.

It seemed that nothing would stand in the way of Baal's supremacy, but there was another powerful influence in the land: the prophet Elijah, who continually confronted Ahab, reminding him of the one true God. Ahab saw Elijah as a troublemaker, disturbing his authority, his way of life. 'Is it you, you troubler of Israel?' he says to him and back comes the reply, 'I have not troubled Israel; but you have, and your father's house, because you have forsaken the commandments of the Lord and followed the Baals' (1 Kings 18:17–18).

Ahab was afraid of Elijah for he recognized that the prophet had a strength and source of power that neither the king nor Jezebel nor all the prophets of Baal had. Read the account of Elijah's triumph by fire and rain and his pronouncement of God's sentence of death on Ahab after the king had ordered the murder of Naboth (1 Kings 17—18 and 21). Ahab may have been king, but he was like a frightened child when faced with the truth. Did he really repent or was he just scared? Ahab knew the truth, but what did he do about it?

Prayer

'Teach me your way, O Lord, that I may walk in your truth; give me an undivided heart to revere your name' (Psalm 86:11).

MC

Wednesday 26 October

2 KINGS 12:2–9 (NRSV, ABRIDGED)

Faithful accounting

Jehoash did what was right in the sight of the Lord all his days, because the priest Jehoiada instructed him... Jehoash said to the priests, 'All the money offered as sacred donations that is brought into the house of the Lord... let the priests receive from each of the donors; and let them repair the house wherever any need of repairs is discovered.' But by the twenty-third year of King Jehoash the priests had made no repairs to the house... Then the priest Jehoiada took a chest, made a hole in its lid, and set it beside the altar on the right side as one entered the house of the Lord; the priests who guarded the threshold put in it all the money that was brought into the house of the Lord.

Jehoash was instrumental in repairing the temple and restoring Israel's religious life. He could be said to be the inventor of the money box, for when his instructions were not followed about using temple offerings for repairs, he ordered that the money should only be used for its designated purpose—hence the security system to make sure it was so. Verse 15 says, 'They did not ask for an account from those into whose hand they delivered the money to pay out to the workers, for they dealt honestly.' The money came in freely and was used wisely for the rebuilding work.

Sadly, after the death of Jehoiada, Jehoash panicked when threatened by a Syrian invasion and took the treasures from the temple and sent them to King Hazael as a bribe to withdraw from Jerusalem (vv. 17–18). He was later assassinated by two of his own trusted officers—a sorry end to his reign (vv. 20–21).

Money boxes of all kinds are still useful for setting aside cash for a particular purpose. Notice how many are in churches, securely protected from 'helping hands' and labelled so you know where and how the donations will be used. More importantly, our reading today reminds us of the need to be good stewards of all that we have and give generously and from a full and loving heart for the extension of God's kingdom.

Reflection
'For where your treasure is, there your heart will be also'
(Luke 12:34).

MC

The price of prosperity

In the fifteenth year of King Amaziah... of Judah, King Jeroboam son of Joash of Israel began to reign in Samaria; he reigned for forty-one years. He did what was evil in the sight of the Lord; he did not depart from all the sins of Jeroboam son of Nebat... He restored the border of Israel from Lebo-hamath as far as the Sea of the Arabah... Now the rest of the acts of Jeroboam, and all that he did, and his might, how he fought, and how he recovered for Israel Damascus and Hamath, which had belonged to Judah, are they not written in the Book of the Annals of the Kings of Israel?

Here was a king who was powerful indeed. Under him, there was great economic prosperity. The kingdom was extended during a time of wealth, security and grandeur on a huge scale. The picture looked so good—until viewed from another perspective, which is that of the ordinary people at the bottom of the pile. A veneer of glory covered misery and hypocrisy, but could not disguise the true situation from God or his faithful prophet Amos.

The book of Amos exposes the true picture and pronounces God's judgment: '... they sell the righteous for silver, and the needy for a pair of sandals—they... trample the head of the poor into the dust of the earth, and push the afflicted out of the way' (Amos 2:6–7) and 'I hate, I despise your festivals, and I take no delight in your solemn assemblies. Even though you offer me your burnt offerings and grain offerings, I will not accept them' (Amos 5:21–22).

Jeroboam paid no heed to the warnings. After all, he felt secure—he had brought prosperity to his people, won back territory, built a splendid fortress city and luxurious houses. Religious observance seemingly flourished and so did the king—for 41 years—so who would bother to take notice of a shepherd prophet called Amos?

Time went on and everything was fine—or so it seemed. Time caught up with Jeroboam at last, however, as it does with all men and women. He died and, within 25 years, the nation collapsed, its great places destroyed and its people taken captive and scattered (2 Kings 17:5–23).

Reflection

What is my security built on: human endeavour or God's promises?

MC

An abundance of blessings

[Hezekiah] commanded the people who lived in Jerusalem to give the portion due to the priests and the Levites, so that they might devote themselves to the Law of the Lord. As soon as the word spread, the people of Israel gave in abundance the first fruits of grain, wine, honey, and of all the produce of the field; and they brought in abundantly the tithe of everything… When Hezekiah and the officials came and saw the heaps, they blessed the Lord and his people Israel… And every work that he undertook in the service of the house of God, and in accordance with the Law, and the commandments, to seek his God, he did with all his heart; and he prospered.

'Come, ye thankful people, come, raise the song of harvest-home.' No doubt many of us will be singing this as we join in harvest celebrations, praising God for physical, material and spiritual blessings. In our reading today, we have a picture of people coming joyfully into the temple, laden with their first fruits to offer to God, to provide for their spiritual leaders, in obedience to the Law.

King Hezekiah was one of the outstanding kings of Israel. His name, meaning 'Yahweh is my strength', described perfectly this God-fearing, God-loving good man, whose whole life was centred on God and serving his people. He thoroughly eradicated evil and heathen practices, renewed the covenant with God and re-established the Levites and priests to lead and teach the people in the restored temple so that worship could begin again. Under his leadership, the people prospered, they were brought back into the experience of being God's people and learned the joy of obedience and service.

Hezekiah set the example and maintained that witness before his people, acting always in the spirit of thanksgiving to God and acknowledging that it was God who reigned above all other kings, all other powers. We should pray that God will raise up leaders in our world like Hezekiah, so that all people may know peace and prosperity and learn to give thanks to God.

Sunday reflection

'Then all the people said "Amen!" and praised the Lord' (1 Chronicles 16:36). Today, as we come to worship, may we make an offering of thanksgiving and praise that overflows in blessings to those around us.

MC

2 Chronicles 26:1–5, 16–21 (NRSV, abridged)

Pride that destroys

Then all the people of Judah took Uzziah, who was sixteen years old, and made him king to succeed his father Amaziah... he reigned for fifty-two years in Jerusalem... He did what was right in the sight of the Lord, just as his father Amaziah had done. He set himself to seek God in the days of Zechariah, who instructed him in the fear of God; and as long as he sought the Lord, God made him prosper... But when he had become strong he grew proud, to his destruction. For he was false to the Lord his God, and entered the temple of the Lord to make offering on the altar of incense... and when he became angry with the priests a leprous disease broke out on his forehead... King Uzziah was leprous to the day of his death.

King at 16, a secure family background, the prophet Zechariah as spiritual adviser—Uzziah had every advantage. He dedicated himself to knowing and following the Lord. Everything he did prospered, whether it was defeating enemies or building up his own kingdom. Architect, farmer, water engineer, a fine brain, a superb organizer, he became famous not only in his own kingdom but far beyond it. He was fortunate to be surrounded by good people and we are told that 'he was marvellously helped until he became strong' (v. 15).

Perhaps he took all that help for granted. Maybe he thought that he had done it all himself because he became a proud man, thinking that nothing was beyond his power, his capability and his right. Then he overstepped the mark, going into the temple and taking on himself the role of the priest.

The priest Azariah, with a large company of fellow priests, tried to stop him, but Uzziah would not listen and ranted and raved at them (vv. 17–19). As he did so, he became leprous. For the rest of his reign he was excluded from his palace, the worshipping community and governing. All that he loved and had worked for was taken from him, but he had only himself to blame. Rebellious pride is the very root of sin and throughout scripture we have constant warnings of its consequences.

Reflection

'When pride comes, then comes disgrace; but wisdom is with the humble' (Proverbs 11:2).

MC

2 KINGS 24:8, 12; 25:27–30 (NRSV, ABRIDGED)

Kindness and mercy

Jehoiachin was eighteen years old when he began to reign; he reigned three months in Jerusalem... King Jehoiachin... gave himself up to the king of Babylon, himself, his mother, his servants, his officers and his palace officials... King Evil-merodach of Babylon, in the year that he began to reign, released King Jehoiachin of Judah from prison; he spoke kindly to him, and gave him a seat above the other seats of the kings who were with him in Babylon. So Jehoiachin put aside his prison clothes. Every day of his life he dined regularly in the king's presence... a regular allowance was given him by the king, a portion every day, as long as he lived.

He hadn't a chance, this 18-year-old, against the might of Nebuchadnezzar, King of Babylon. So, he gave himself up into captivity, along with his family, the influential and strong men of Judah, his own treasures and those of the temple. Only the poorest people were left in the land, which was considered of no use to Babylon (24:14).

This was the way of the world then—survival of the fittest, winner takes all. Cruel and barbaric practices were the norm; no one expected mercy, nor did they show it to others. As we look around our world, we still see in many places a vicious cycle of hatred, violence, oppression and degradation, generating enmity between individuals and nations, offering no hope to weaker and more vulnerable people.

Yet, here in our reading, we do have a sign of hope in an act of compassion. Nebuchadnezzar's successor, King Evil-merodach, not only released Jehoiachin from prison but also restored his honour and dignity, showing him friendship and providing for him for the rest of his life. After 37 years in prison, Jehoiachin must have given up any hope of release, but here was an outstretched hand, lifting him up and out. In a seemingly hopeless situation, goodness and mercy shone through, bringing release and a measure of restoration.

It reminds me of the story Jesus told in answer to the question 'Who is my neighbour?' (Luke 10:25–37) and of his challenge to 'Go and do likewise'. This is surely a message to each one of us.

Sunday prayer

Use me, Lord, as an agent of your love and compassion to someone in need today.

MC

2 Chronicles 33:10–13 (NRSV)

There is always hope

The Lord spoke to Manasseh and to his people, but they gave no heed. Therefore the Lord brought against them the commanders of the army of the king of Assyria, who took Manasseh captive in manacles, bound him with fetters, and brought him to Babylon. While he was in distress he entreated the favour of the Lord his God and humbled himself greatly before the God of his ancestors. He prayed to him, and God received his entreaty, heard his plea, and restored him again to Jerusalem and to his kingdom. Then Manasseh knew that the Lord indeed was God.

Manasseh was a thoroughly nasty piece of work. Fascinated by heathen cults and religions, he did everything possible to wipe out the worship of God. He practised sorcery, allied himself with wizards and mediums and forced his sons to go through heathen rites (vv. 2–9). He led his people astray, causing them to follow his evil example, until the whole country was depraved and defiled. Defiantly and arrogantly, he undid all the good that his father Hezekiah had done. However, a day of reckoning came when he was taken captive into Babylon as, in his anguish, he cried to God to help him, humbly throwing himself on the mercy of the one he had despised and rejected. Would you or I have listened to him? God, though, graciously saved and restored him.

As for Manasseh, he sought to undo the evil that he had done. He restored the altar of the Lord, took away all the images and high places he had made and ordered his people to return 'to serve the Lord the God of Israel' (v. 16).

Maybe there are those we despair of, feeling that they have gone so far from God that there is no hope for them. Perhaps Manasseh can remind us that there is always hope, even for the most blatant sinner, if they are prepared to come humbly before God, asking for forgiveness. After all, God reaches out to us, doesn't he? Also, 'while we were still sinners Christ died for us' (Romans 5:8).

Reflection

'For the love of God is broader than the measure of man's mind; and the heart of the Eternal is most wonderfully kind' (F.W. Faber, 1854). Praise God for his love and mercy!

MC

2 CHRONICLES 34:1–3, 30–31 (NRSV, ABRIDGED)

Making the word known

Josiah was eight years old when he began to reign; he reigned for thirty-one years in Jerusalem... while he was still a boy, he began to seek the God of his ancestor David... The king went up to the house of the Lord, with... all the people both great and small; he read in their hearing all the words of the book of the covenant that had been found in the house of the Lord. The king stood in his place and made a covenant before the Lord, to follow the Lord, keeping his commandments, his decrees, and his statutes, with all his heart and with all his soul, to perform the words of the covenant that were written in this book.

Josiah set out to purge the land of idolatry and re-establish the worship of the one true God. He began restoring 'the house of the Lord' in Jerusalem (v. 8) and it was while the repair work was going on that the long-forgotten book of the Law was discovered—the book of Deuteronomy—and it was read to the king (vv. 14, 18). The king not only listened to it but also took it to heart and gathered together the inhabitants of Jerusalem so that they could hear it, too.

Recognizing that the words of warning were directed to them— that unless they obeyed the Lord they would perish—Josiah made a solemn covenant before God with all the people that they would serve the Lord wholeheartedly and keep his commandments. It was a renewal of the covenant made on Mount Sinai when God commanded Moses and the people to pledge obedience and service. King Josiah oversaw a great gathering, first of penitence and prayer, then of solemn dedication and celebration. The opening of the word of the Lord led to a new start.

We can thank God that we have his word, and thank God, too, for the work of organizations, such as BRF, that offer help with reading, understanding and obeying the word. May we do our part in living it faithfully and sharing it with others.

Prayer

We bless you, Lord, for all who teach us to love the scriptures, and for all who help us to understand them.

The BRF Story
MC

The wages of sin

In the fourth year of King Jehoiakim son of Josiah of Judah, this word came to Jeremiah from the Lord: 'Take a scroll and write on it all the words that I have spoken to you against Israel and Judah and all the nations… It may be that when the house of Judah hears of all the disasters that I intend to do to them, all of them may turn from their evil ways, so that I may forgive their iniquity and their sin… As Jehudi read three or four columns, the king would cut them off with a penknife and throw them into the fire in the brazier, until the entire scroll was consumed… Yet neither the king, nor any of his servants who heard all these words, was alarmed, nor did they tear their garments.

Here was a king who turned against God's ways. Out of fear he became a servant of King Nebuchadnezzar, but then rebelled, trying to assert himself again (2 Kings 24:1). He would not see how outclassed he was, nor would he accept help from the prophet Jeremiah who urged him to turn humbly to God and ask for forgiveness. He often called for Jeremiah's advice, but never took it and when the words God had given through the prophet were read to him, he destroyed the scroll—thinking no doubt that this would free him from responsibility. His is a sad story of a man who had many chances to turn back to God, but was determined to go his own way. Defeated by King Nebuchadnezzar, he was taken into Babylon in chains and, as Jeremiah had prophesied, met a violent end (2 Chronicles 36:6–8).

How could a son of the great and good King Josiah turn out like this? It was because he chose to go his own way. He was concerned only for his own position, his own skin and he lost both. We may pity or scorn him, but do we always heed wise counsel ourselves? Do we ever close our eyes and hearts to uncomfortable words of scripture?

Prayer

'Teach me, O Lord, the way of your statutes, and I will observe it to the end. Give me understanding, that I may keep your law and observe it with my whole heart'
(Psalm 119:33–34).

MC

2 Chronicles 36:11–13 (NRSV)

The last chance

Zedekiah was twenty-one years old when he began to reign; he reigned for eleven years in Jerusalem. He did what was evil in the sight of the Lord his God. He did not humble himself before the prophet Jeremiah who spoke from the mouth of the Lord. He also rebelled against King Nebuchadnezzar, who had made him swear by God; he stiffened his neck and hardened his heart against turning to the Lord, God of Israel.

The youngest son of Josiah, Zedekiah was placed on the throne by Nebuchadnezzar after Jehoiachin had been taken into Babylon. Not content to be a 'puppet king', he, rebelled and finally lost out against the might of Nebuchadnezzar's forces. Although he escaped, he had to witness the execution of his sons, before having his eyes put out (2 Kings 25:7).

His reign is strikingly and horribly portrayed in the book of Ezekiel, especially in chapters 8, 9 and 22. The pictures of extreme depravity, corrupt religion and moral degeneracy show the depths to which human beings can fall and the resultant misery for all concerned.

Did the king know any better? Did he want anything better? On a number of occasions he asked for advice from Jeremiah the prophet, hoping that there might be a message of hope from God: 'perhaps the Lord will perform a wonderful deed for us, as he has often done…' (Jeremiah 21:2), but the message was one of judgment: 'For I have set my face against this city for evil and not for good, says the Lord: it shall be given into the hands of the king of Babylon, and he shall burn it with fire' (Jeremiah 21:10). This was not the sort of message that Zedekiah wanted to hear, but it was the truth, as he was to discover.

This is a reminder, if we need one, that God cannot and will not tolerate wrongdoing and disregard for his commandments forever. However, there is glorious hope for those who will seek and obey the Lord: 'for you who revere my name the sun of righteousness shall rise, with healing in its wings' (Malachi 4:2)—a promise wonderfully fulfilled in Jesus.

Reflection and rejoicing

'The kingdom of the world has become the kingdom of our Lord and of his Messiah, and he will reign for ever and ever' (Revelation 11:15).

MC

ISAIAH 45:1, 4–6 (NRSV, ABRIDGED)

Subject to higher authority

Thus says the Lord to his anointed, to Cyrus, whose right hand I have grasped to subdue nations before him and strip kings of their robes, to open doors before him—and the gates shall not be closed... I call you by your name, I surname you, though you do not know me. I am the Lord, and there is no other; besides me there is no god. I arm you, though you do not know me, so that they may know, from the rising of the sun and from the west, that there is no one besides me; I am the Lord, and there is no other.

This word of the Lord concerns a king of Persia who would be greatly used in his service. Cyrus himself worshipped heathen gods, but he recognized that people should be free to worship their own god—hence his support of the rebuilding of the temple in Jerusalem (Ezra 1). He also believed that people have the right to live where they choose to live, not where they have been taken to or placed. His reign was of a very different nature from those of others—humane, far-sighted. He was a good servant of God, yet, paradoxically, remained a pagan king.

What influenced Cyrus? Was it his nature, the prayers of God's people or God choosing to work through this king, pointing the way to the one who would be the means of salvation for the whole world? It was probably a combination of many things, but it shows us that God uses whomever he chooses to reveal his glory. As it says in our reading today, 'I am the Lord, and there is no other' (v. 5).

Paul urged that 'supplications, prayers, intercessions and thanksgivings' be made 'for everyone, for kings and all who are in high positions, so that we may lead a quiet and peaceable life in all godliness and dignity' (1 Timothy 2:1–2). Remember Cyrus and the words of Paul as you come to worship this Sunday.

Reflection

Those in positions of leadership have not only privileges, but also high, sometimes impossible, demands placed on them. Pray that they might have the wisdom and integrity, courage and compassion, strength and humility to carry out their responsibilities.

MC

DANIEL 6:25–27 (NRSV)

The lion king

Then King Darius wrote to all peoples and nations of every language throughout the whole world: 'May you have abundant prosperity! I make a decree, that in all my royal dominion people should tremble and fear before the God of Daniel: For he is the living God, enduring for ever. His kingdom shall never be destroyed, and his dominion has no end. He delivers and rescues, he works signs and wonders in heaven and on earth; for he has saved Daniel from the power of the lions.'

The story of Daniel in the lions' den is a familiar one and you can read it in Daniel chapter 6. Darius was a man of integrity and honour—he kept his word, even when it seemed that it would bring him great personal sadness. Having signed an edict condemning anyone who worshipped any god besides him to being thrown into the den of lions, he spent a sleepless night worrying about Daniel's fate, but in the morning joyfully acknowledged the power of Daniel's god to save where he could not.

When he received a letter from a provincial governor, telling him that the Jews had no authority to rebuild the temple, he ordered a search of the archives to find out whether or not Cyrus had ordered the rebuilding. Discovering that Cyrus had issued such a decree, Darius renewed the order and also authorized the return of the looted treasures to the temple. He replied to the governor in no uncertain terms, saying, 'keep away; let the work on this house of God alone' (Ezra 6:6–7).

He not only ordered the work to continue unhindered, but also that the cost should be met, sacrifices provided and no one should impede the rebuilding, on pain of death (Ezra 6:8–11). This was no grudging acknowledgment, but wholehearted support and approval.

Darius was a powerful ruler, but he was also a seeker after truth. Through Darius, God's word and work went forward, God's people were blessed and enabled once again to worship in the rebuilt temple and live in peace and security. Darius was an instrument of the Lord, willing and wholehearted.

Prayer

Lord God, may we always be eager to seek the truth, and in finding it to follow it, giving you the glory, and acknowledging your authority in our lives.

MC

Psalms 42—72

When a good book or film comes out, we all then wait expectantly for the sequel. This book—Psalms 42 to 72—is 'Psalms 2' and in some ways is similar to the book that went before it, in other ways different. Two of the psalms—53 and 70—are almost exact duplicates of psalms in book 1 (14 and 40:13–17), but the name for God, 'Yahweh' (written as Lord), is used fewer times than in book 1 and, instead, the term 'Elohim' (God Almighty) is used. Although we do not know the reason for this, it may be because, in some circles, the name Yahweh was considered too holy to use.

Like book 1, book 2 closes with a sentence of praise (72:18–19; compare 41:13) and the statement that 'the prayers of David son of Jesse are ended'. There are, however, more psalms attributed to David later in the book of Psalms as a whole. This collection was obviously self-contained at the time.

Unlike the headings applied to most chapters of the Bible, the headings in Psalms are original. In this book, only 71 is without a heading (note that Psalm 43 has no heading as it was originally one psalm with 42). These headings point us to the inspiration and subject matter of each psalm. Indeed, some of the psalms of David refer to specific incidents in his life, which are clearly reflected in the subject matter of the psalm. The headings also sometimes give musical directions, often using terms the meanings of which are now unclear to us.

However, if some of the origins and original musical settings have been lost, the subject matter of the psalms never goes out of date. Now as then we can use them to bring to God our different feelings and circumstances, for the psalms do not just reflect the way that we feel worship should be, but the way life really is, bringing God into every part of life, coming before him no matter how we are feeling. Jesus used the psalms to show not only how they spoke prophetically about him (compare John 15:25 and Psalm 69:4) but also in his own prayer (compare Luke 23:46 and Psalm 31:5). In various forms, they have always been used by Christians in worship (Colossians 3:16) and we can use them ourselves, not only in study but also to bring to God things that our own words often struggle to express.

Jane Cornish

Psalm 42:1, 3–5 (NRSV)

A God-shaped hole

As a deer longs for flowing streams, so my soul longs for you, O God... My tears have been my food day and night, while people say to me continually, 'Where is your God?' These things I remember, as I pour out my soul: how I went with the throng, and led them in procession to the house of God, with glad shouts and songs of thanksgiving, a multitude keeping festival. Why are you cast down, O my soul, and why are you disquieted within me? Hope in God; for I shall again praise him, my help and my God.

As the opening song in a hymn-book, this psalm is not perhaps as upbeat as we would expect! The 'glad shouts and songs of thanksgiving' (v. 4) are much more usual. Few of us could say, however, that we have not experienced what the psalmist is talking about.

There are times for everyone when God seems remote. For the psalmist, it is because he is so far from the temple. The psalm may have been written in exile—a difficult experience for a people whose faith was so bound up with the land that God had given and the temple where his glory dwelt—yet he is not prepared to give up. Though God seems far away, he is still very real to the psalmist in that, without God, he knows that something is missing from his life. His apparent absence leaves a big gap.

On the wall of a concentration camp someone wrote, 'I believe in the sun, even when it is not shining; I believe in love, even when I cannot feel it; I believe in God, even when he is silent.' It does not take such extreme circumstances for us to feel sometimes that God is remote. The psalmist, however, holds on to the fact that God has not changed and, if he is not feeling good, he tells God so. God does not want us to pretend, neither does he want us to shut him out. He knows what it is to be lonely, to feel cut off (Matthew 27:46). He is the rock that is dependable, even when everything else in our lives is shifting (Psalm 42:9).

Sunday prayer

Lord, help us to trust in your presence, even when we feel alone.

JC

More than conquerors

We have heard with our ears, O God; our fathers have told us what you did in their days, in days long ago... But now you have rejected and humbled us; you no longer go out with our armies... All this happened to us, though we had not forgotten you or been false to your covenant. Our hearts had not turned back; our feet had not strayed from your path. But you crushed us and made us a haunt for jackals and covered us over with deep darkness... Awake, O Lord! Why do you sleep? Rouse yourself! Do not reject us for ever. Why do you hide your face and forget our misery and oppression?

If the writer of Psalm 42 draws strength from remembering the good times, the writer of this psalm does not find them quite so encouraging. Sometimes it can be like that, particularly when the good times are happening to somebody else. The wonderful testimonies we hear in church, the uplifting Christian biographies with their tales of triumph in adversity—these can just serve to point up the contrast with our own situation. They can even make us feel guilty. We can think that, if things are not working out, it must be our fault. The psalmist knows that this is not the problem (vv. 17–19), so what is going on?

We can feel anger towards God, too. Why are you letting this happen, God? Don't you care? Responding like this to situations can also make us feel guilty. Should we be speaking to God like this? The psalmist does not hesitate, though, saying, 'Awake... Rouse yourself!' (v. 23). True prayer is about bringing to God how we really feel and what is really happening. Whether it is trouble in our life that is bothering us or the state of the world, faith is not about pretending that everything is all right. It is better to turn towards God with our problems than let them drive us away from him. Despite the psalmist's bafflement, he still comes to God in worship (v. 8) and believes that he is ultimately in control.

The psalm ends with the words 'your unfailing love' (v. 26) and this is what we can hold on to in every situation, as we shall see in tomorrow's reading.

Reflection

Read Romans 8:28–39 and thank God that he knows what we are going through.

JC

When storms strike

God is our refuge and strength, a very present help in trouble. Therefore we will not fear, though the earth should change, though the mountains shake in the heart of the sea; though its waters roar and foam, though the mountains tremble with its tumult... The nations are in an uproar, the kingdoms totter; he utters his voice, the earth melts... 'Be still, and know that I am God! I am exalted among the nations, I am exalted in the earth.'

When a storm hits, we need somewhere safe to go. We're not talking about wind and rain but the sort of storm that knocks our lives sideways—illness, bereavement, disaster. It's important to know where to turn because, suddenly, the whole foundations of our lives can be knocked from under us.

This psalmist knows about trouble. He finds in God what he needs: a safe refuge, strength, help. What does the psalm tell us about what this means in practice?

First, we should be prepared (v. 1). There may well be storms and difficulties in our lives. God does not remove all troubles from us, but he is there with us when life is difficult.

Second, we know who we can trust (v. 7). Our confidence in the God we have seen at work in the past and who has promised to be with us in the future gives us hope in the worst situation. It gives us trust even if our world seems to be collapsing around us.

Last, we know who's in charge (v. 10). It may not seem that this is true when we look at the world today—we see the suffering and feel helpless—but for Jesus the way of victory was the way of the cross and we, too, are called to trust, even in the most apparently hopeless situations, that God is at work. Jesus has gone before us and in him we can go forward confidently when there seems no hope.

For individuals everywhere facing hardship, grief, illness, there are no easy answers. There are Christians all over the world, however, who have trusted in God and who can testify that he is a refuge and strength in all sorts of storms.

Reflection

Pray for someone you know who is facing storms in their life at the moment.

JC

Right priorities

Great is the Lord, and most worthy of praise, in the city of our God, his holy mountain. It is beautiful in its loftiness, the joy of the whole earth… When the kings joined forces, when they advanced together, they saw her and were astounded; they fled in terror… Walk about Zion, go around her, count her towers, consider well her ramparts, view her citadels, that you may tell of them to the next generation. For this God is our God for ever and ever; he will be our guide even to the end.

What do you look for in a good church service? Some like candles and incense, some prefer guitars and dancing. You may like the majestic grandeur of a formal sung liturgy or prefer something simpler, more contemporary. For the psalmist here, location was all-important. The worship of God was bound up for him with the city of Jerusalem. This psalm might have been used on a march round the city, which reflects for the worshippers the greatness of God.

There are many things that help us to worship God and it is not wrong to worship him in a way that comes naturally to us. Just as lovers associate particular times, places or songs with their love, so we find certain things special because they speak to us of the love and greatness of God. This is how the psalmist feels about Jerusalem.

The trouble comes when the way of worshipping becomes more important than God himself. For some people in Jerusalem, the place became so bound up with the worship of God that they found it difficult to see how they could worship him anywhere else (Psalm 137). If we become dependent on a particular sort of service or style of music or type of building or anything else, then there will come a time when that is not there any more, so we have to make a change. What we need to remember at that point is the God who is behind it all, who is worshipped not so much in any one place or any one way as 'in spirit and truth' (John 4:23).

Reflection

Try going to a type of service with which you are unfamiliar, to see how people find God in different ways.

JC

Thursday 10 November

PSALM 50:1, 4, 7, 21 (NIV)

In the dock

The Mighty One, God, the Lord, speaks and summons the earth from the rising of the sun to the place where it sets… He summons the heavens above, and the earth, that he may judge his people… 'Hear, O my people, and I will speak, O Israel, and I will testify against you: I am God, your God… These things you have done and I kept silent; you thought I was altogether like you. But I will rebuke you and accuse you to your face.'

It's a twist worthy of the best detective drama. The case seems all sewn up and the detective swings round to the person we least expect and says, 'You are guilty!' The scene imagined in this psalm is a heavenly court and God summons the Earth to account. Israel is confident of the outcome (v. 3): God is just and there is plenty wrong in the nations. He will surely put things right. In the very next verse, however, the tables are turned—God's judgment is against his people! They are neglecting their covenant with him (v. 5) and disobeying the heart of the law (vv. 18–20).

It is too easy to move from confidence to complacency, from pledging ourselves to be on God's side, to believing that he is on ours, thinking that God is like us (v. 21), sharing our prejudices and preferences, taking his patience for tacit approval. Today, too, there is plenty wrong in the world and we rightly bring it before God, but what we fail to see is the way in which we ourselves share in those problems. Like the older son in the parable (Luke 15:11–32), we can believe that we're the ones who have got it all right, and God really ought to be pleased with us. On the contrary, Jesus reminds us, the very fact that we have heard God's word means that we have a greater responsibility to live in the way that he wants us to. From everyone who has been given much, much will be demanded and from the one who has been entrusted with much, much more will be asked (Luke 12:48). Being the people of God means being called to holiness, not immunity from prosecution.

Prayer

Lord, thank you for your call. Help us to live lives worthy of you and of your calling.

JC

Ritual and reality

I have no need of a bull from your stall or of goats from your pens, for every animal of the forest is mine, and the cattle on a thousand hills... If I were hungry I would not tell you, for the world is mine, and all that is in it... Sacrifice thank offerings to God, fulfil your vows to the Most High, and call upon me in the day of trouble; I will deliver you, and you will honour me... You do not delight in sacrifice, or I would bring it; you do not take pleasure in burnt offerings.

As we saw yesterday, God continually calls his people into relationship with him. At the heart of that relationship, as a way of mending and maintaining it, was the system of sacrifice. The books of the Law are full of precise instructions for what must be sacrificed when, for each occasion in life and worship. Sometimes, however, the prophets had to remind the people why they did it. Sacrifice had to be matched by a real submission and obedience to God (1 Samuel 15:20–23; Hosea 6:6).

The point the psalmist and the prophets are making is not that they thought the sacrifices were wrong. They understood that they were God's way of demonstrating the seriousness of sin and, as a sign of repentance, they had real value. Rather, they were saying that when we think that we can buy God's forgiveness by acting in a particular way, whether by sacrifices of some kind or going to church or giving to charity or giving up chocolate for Lent, it is a waste of time. There is nothing we can do to earn the love of the God. Whatever we do for God, the point is to focus on why we are doing it. God does not need our help—he does not want sacrifices because he is hungry or prayers because he cannot act without them. Again and again, God calls his people into relationship, which means that what he wants is for us to come to him in love and grateful dependence on all he does for us, accepting his free gift of forgiveness and relationship restored, bringing our offerings because we love him and not out of a misguided notion that he somehow needs us to do so.

Prayer
*Thank you, Lord, for your
unconditional love.*

JC

Coming clean

Have mercy on me, O God, according to your steadfast love; according to your abundant mercy blot out my transgressions. Wash me thoroughly from my iniquity, and cleanse me from my sin… Create in me a clean heart, O God, and put a new and right spirit within me. Do not cast me away from your presence, and do not take your holy spirit from me… The sacrifice acceptable to God is a broken spirit; a broken and contrite heart, O God, you will not despise.

What makes you feel good about yourself? Image is very important in our society, so people try to find a sense of self-worth in sports, diet, looks, career, moving in the 'right' circles. The trouble is, we can seldom live up to the image we try to portray. Sooner or later it is likely to all fall apart.

The sad tale of adultery, murder and lies behind this psalm is recounted in 2 Samuel 11 and 12. Here, David recognizes his actions for exactly what they were—sin—and brings them to God.

It's sometimes said that Christians have no sense of self-worth because they are always thinking about sin. David, however, comes to God precisely because he knows that, whatever he has done, he still has worth in God's eyes. All is not lost because God cares about him.

A preacher once offered his congregation a crisp new £20 note. As you can imagine, every-body wanted it. Then he crumpled it up, stamped on it and held it up again, creased and dirty. 'Who wants it now?' he asked. Of course they still did. When we sin, it spoils God's image in us, but the image is still there. We are still worth just the same as before and God still wants us. So, when David talks about God requiring us to have a broken spirit, a broken and contrite heart, he does not mean that God wants to subdue us or humiliate us. What is necessary is that we learn to depend on him. The attitude that says, 'I can manage by myself', 'I'm all right', 'I'll deal with this my way' stops anybody—including God—helping us and he does not force help on anybody.

Prayer

Thank you, Lord, that you love me for what I am, not what I would like to be.

JC

The lessons of history

Shout with joy to God, all the earth! Sing the glory of his name; make his praise glorious!… Come and see what God has done, how awesome his works on man's behalf! He turned the sea into dry land, they passed through the waters on foot—come, let us rejoice in him… Praise our God, O peoples, let the sound of his praise be heard; he has preserved our lives and kept our feet from slipping. For you, O God, tested us; you refined us like silver. You brought us into prison and laid burdens on our backs. You let men ride over our heads; we went through fire and water, but you brought us to a place of abundance.

At the time of writing, I have just returned from a reunion of our church youth group, 30 years on! Apart from the opportunity to catch up with people, it was a good reminder of how the group had been such a good foundation for us in our Christian lives. Many have continued in the faith that they had been growing then, thanks to the dedication of the leaders and the encouragement we were able to give each other. The past plays a big part in making us what we are.

In this psalm, the second of four (65—68) described as 'songs' and used at festivals, the psalmist reflects on Israel's past and how God has been at work in it and continues to work still. He does not restrict his memories to the good times because he recognizes that God is at work in painful experiences, too—something we can often only see as we look back on them.

As we come to Remembrance Sunday, we recall the past events that have shaped us and others, even if we were not directly involved. As we worship the God of history, let's thank him for his presence in all the events, both pleasant and painful, that go to make up our past and the past of our nation. Let's give thanks for all the people whose dedication and commitment have helped us to be the people and the nation we are today.

Sunday reflection

Is there someone you can identify as having a decisive influence on your Christian life? Thank God for them now.

JC

A blessing for whom?

Clap your hands, all you nations; shout to God with cries of joy. How awesome is the Lord Most High, the great King over all the earth! He subdued nations under us, peoples under our feet. He chose our inheritance for us, the pride of Jacob, whom he loved... God reigns over the nations; God is seated on his holy throne. The nobles of the nations assemble as the people of the God of Abraham, for the kings of the earth belong to God; he is greatly exalted.

We find a strange juxtaposition of ideas in this psalm, which describes the nations being called on to praise the God who has helped Israel to subdue them! However those nations may have reacted, the people of God can discern two important truths about God in this psalm of worship. He is God of the whole world and he has, in some important sense, chosen one particular group of people to be his own.

The statement that God chose a particular people in history and that we as the Church are chosen by God now is not one that is well received in today's pluralistic society. Why should God favour one group if he is the God of the whole world?

The truth is that if God chooses certain people, whether a nation or individuals, he chooses them not so that they may feel superiority over others, but in order that he may bless others through them.

We are called to serve, to be the agents of God's mission of love to the whole world. It is significant that the psalmist mentions Abraham as, when God chose him, he chose to bless him, to make him into a nation and make his name great. For what purpose? In order that he would be a blessing to others: 'all peoples on earth will be blessed through you', he told him (Genesis 12:3).

We can thank God for his blessings and first among them is that he has called us to know him, love and serve him. We come not in arrogance that we are chosen, but in humility and the knowledge that we are called, in his name, to be a blessing to others.

Reflection

How can I be a blessing to others today?

JC

The fool

The fool says in his heart, 'There is no God.' They are corrupt, and their ways are vile; there is no one who does good. God looks down from heaven on the sons of men to see if there are any who understand, any who seek God. Everyone has turned away, they have together become corrupt; there is no one who does good, not even one. Will the evildoers never learn—those who devour my people as men eat bread and who do not call on God?

As Christians we may occasionally (or frequently) find that the credibility of our faith is challenged: 'How can an intelligent person believe such things?' Sometimes the questioner has not considered the claims of Christianity seriously; sometimes they have thought long and hard. That is not the sort of person the psalmist is talking about. The subject of verse 1 is not deciding that God does not exist; it is more a statement of defiance. He has decided to live his life without reference to God and his values. His lifestyle is one of corruption and exploitation rather than doing good.

David met just such a man in his time of fleeing from Saul. Psalms 52 and 54 have headings indicating that they refer to this time (see 1 Samuel 22; 26). In between these two incidents (chapter 25) comes one that could well lie behind this psalm—when David meets Nabal. Nabal means 'fool' and we see him behaving in just the way this psalm describes. His foolishness comes from the fact that he knows the right way to act (in this case helping David as the Lord's anointed king), but chooses to go his own way instead.

Jesus stressed that living wisely is not about being highly educated or knowing all the answers to life's questions, but living in a way that is consistent with our faith. If we profess belief in a holy, just and loving God, then this will make a difference to our priorities, our decisions, the way we treat others. Building our whole lives on our belief, Jesus tells us, is indeed the wise thing to do (Matthew 7:24–27).

Reflection

If our lifestyle tells others about what we really believe, then the best way to share our faith is to live it!
(Matthew 5:16)

JC

PSALM 55:1, 4, 6, 8, 16, 22 (NRSV)

Get me out of here!

Give ear to my prayer, O God; do not hide yourself from my supplication... My heart is in anguish within me, the terrors of death have fallen upon me... And I say, 'O that I had wings like a dove! I would fly away and be at rest... I would hurry to find a shelter for myself from the raging wind and tempest.' ... But I call upon God, and the Lord will save me... Cast your burden on the Lord, and he will sustain you; he will never permit the righteous to be moved.

There are times when we want to be somewhere else, anywhere but where we are. Our situation is so painful or embarrassing or the problem so intractable that the best solution seems to be to get out fast. Jacob did it (Genesis 27) Elijah did it (1 Kings 19), Jesus' disciples did it (Mark 14:50). Sometimes it is necessary to get out of the way until a situation cools down, but, in the end, all these individuals had to face up to what was bothering them. Running away is rarely a solution.

The psalmist either finds that he cannot flee or resists the impulse. Instead, he calls on God (v. 16) and finds in him the answer to his troubles. He knows that God will sustain him (v. 22), so that even though the circumstances do not change, his ability to cope will.

Often our response to a difficult situation is to pray, 'Lord, get me out of here!' Sometimes God does just that, but at other times we are in the very place God intends us to be. Then, we need to pray for his help to cope, as Jesus did in the garden of Gethsemane (Matthew 26:39). There are many situations that we just cannot face alone, but God will equip us to be in the place he wants, to face up to what scares us, do his will. He will give us not wings like doves, to escape, but wings like eagles (Isaiah 40:31), to rise above our trouble, see a situation from his perspective, be strengthened to carry on.

Reflection

'As for me, I trust in you' (v. 23, NIV). Pray that God will help you to do just this, whatever the circumstances!

JC

Betrayed!

If an enemy were insulting me, I could endure it; if a foe were raising himself against me, I could hide from him. But it is you, a man like myself, my companion, my close friend, with whom I once enjoyed sweet fellowship as we walked with the throng at the house of God... My companion attacks his friends; he violates his covenant. His speech is smooth as butter, yet war is in his heart; his words are more soothing than oil, yet they are drawn swords.

When life is hard, we look to our friends for comfort and support, so when someone we thought we could trust betrays us or lets us down, it is very hard to take. The psalmist, though, is able to come to God with confidence, because he knows that, whatever he is going through and whoever lets him down, God will always be there for him.

As we turn to God feeling the pain of betrayal, we know that he understands what we are going through because God knows what it feels like to be betrayed. The story of the people of God in the Old Testament is a continually repeated saga of God reaching out to his people in loving relationship and his people turning away, betraying his trust (Hosea 11:1–4) as cruelly as a child who rejects their parent despite the care and sacrifice involved in their upbringing. In a parable, Jesus relates how God, the vineyard owner, sent his servants to his people and, as they were rejected one after the other, he then sent his son (Matthew 21:33–41). We know how the Son was betrayed and abandoned by those closest to him.

The experience of betrayal can make us cynical and hard. Like the psalmist, we can react by lashing out, expecting God to take our side as the injured party against those who hurt us. However, the God who knows what it is like to be betrayed has shown us another way—the way of forgiveness. He offers it to us and calls on us to offer it to others.

Reflection

Have you experienced a relationship spoiled by wrongs on one side or the other? Take it to God now and ask him to bring his reconciliation to it. You may need to think what action you have to take, too!

JC

A cry for vengeance

Do you rulers indeed speak justly? Do you judge uprightly among men? No, in your heart you devise injustice, and your hands mete out violence on the earth... Break the teeth in their mouths, O God; tear out, O Lord, the fangs of the lions!... Like a slug melting away as it moves along, like a stillborn child, may they not see the sun... The righteous will be glad when they are avenged, when they bathe their feet in the blood of the wicked. Then men will say, 'Surely the righteous still are rewarded; surely there is a God who judges the earth.'

It is sometimes difficult to come to terms with the tone of the psalms. Earlier we saw how the psalmist did not hesitate to bring his feelings of anger at God into his worship and here he is just as forthright about his desire for vengeance. It makes us wonder how we can use this and similar psalms in our worship.

Just think, however, about certain difficult things. For example, knowing that we need to forgive those who sin against us is not the same as believing we will never feel hurt and angry or that we must leave such feelings behind when we come to God in prayer. At times like these, we can learn from the psalmist's impassioned words. Behind them lies a passion for justice, which comes from a real care for those who are hurt by the sin of others. A saying attributed to philosopher Edmund Burke states that for evil to triumph, all that is necessary is for good men to do nothing.

Our response to the evil we see in the world may not be a cry for vengeance, but there must be outrage at the suffering it causes. 'Is it nothing to you, all you who pass by?' asks the author of Lamentations (1:12). Is our reluctance to share the psalmist's sentiments a commendable love for humanity at its worst, a desire to overcome evil with good or merely a silence born of indifference? The person who remains unmoved at the sufferings of our fellow human beings at the hands of others is surely less in touch with God than the one who cries out for God to act!

Reflection

Does the injustice and suffering we see every day move us to prayer and, when appropriate, action? If not, why not?

JC

Resting in God

Find rest, O my soul, in God alone; my hope comes from him. He alone is my rock and my salvation; he is my fortress, I shall not be shaken… Lowborn men are but a breath, the highborn are but a lie; if weighed on a balance, they are nothing; together they are only a breath. Do not trust in extortion or take pride in stolen goods; though your riches increase, do not set your heart on them.

Ours is not a restful society. Despite labour-saving devices, faster travel and instant communication, most people seem to be in a hurry most of the time. Alongside this busyness is a lack of contentment, a constant desire for a better lifestyle, an ambition to achieve. It is a desire that is hard to satisfy. Of course the advertisers who suggest that their product alone is the answer are seeking not to satisfy our desire but feed it, make us want more and ever more, to carry on a cycle of consumption leading not to satisfaction but, instead, further restlessness.

According to the psalmist, the problem is that we are looking in the wrong place. It's no use being a social climber in order to get a better lifestyle. It's no use shunning high society and hoping for the revolution. Crime isn't going to change your life for the better and, even if you get rich legitimately, wealth is not going to give you everything your heart desires. The only answer to the longing in our hearts, the restlessness that keeps us looking for something that satisfies once and for all, is God. 'You have made us for yourself,' said Augustine, 'and our hearts are restless till they find their rest in you.'

It is not wrong to have ambition. There is nothing sinful about saving for a new car or a bigger house, but we need to ask ourselves 'What is the driving force in my life?' The thing that is really important to us, Jesus warns, will determine where our heart is (Matthew 6:21), what we do and what we make our priorities. Only when God is central in our lives—the first in our hearts—will we find in him the end of our searching, the rest that conquers our restlessness.

Reflection

Try to spend some time with God away from the busyness of life.

JC

Live it!

O God, you are my God, earnestly I seek you; my soul thirsts for you, my body longs for you, in a dry and weary land where there is no water... Because your love is better than life, my lips will glorify you. I will praise you as long as I live, and in your name I will lift up my hands. My soul will be satisfied as with the richest of foods; with singing lips my mouth will praise you. On my bed I remember you; I think of you through the watches of the night. Because you are my help, I sing in the shadow of your wings.

'He eats, drinks and sleeps it' is how people often describe those with a real passion for something. These are the kinds of terms that the psalmist uses to tell of his longing for God in this psalm (vv. 1, 5, 6). The heading tells us that the psalm was written by David in the desert of Judah, where he would have been all too well aware of how necessary water is for life. He is not just concerned with physical needs here, however; God, he declares, is equally vital to his well-being.

We are often told to drink more water to stay healthy, but when we are not in a desert, it is easy to underestimate our body's need for it. We become dehydrated without even realizing it. Just like we need water, we need God, whether we are aware that we do or not. If we are to be spiritually healthy, we need to keep coming back to God to be refreshed.

Like learning to drink more water, there are ways in which we can learn to seek God more. As we spend time with him in prayer and worship, as the psalmist did, even when perhaps we don't feel like it, as we look to him to be the answer to our needs—and to be even more important to us than any of those needs (v. 3)—we will find that he is the one who satisfies our soul, even in the deserts of our lives.

Sunday reflection

Jesus told the Samaritan woman that he could give her a 'spring of water welling up to eternal life' (John 4:14). Let us pray with her, 'give us this water'.

JC

A harvest blessing

May God be gracious to us and bless us and make his face to shine upon us, that your way may be known upon earth, your saving power among all nations. Let the peoples praise you, O God; let all the peoples praise you. Let the nations be glad and sing for joy, for you judge the peoples with equity and guide the nations upon earth. Let the peoples praise you, O God; let all the peoples praise you. The earth has yielded its increase; God, our God, has blessed us. May God continue to bless us; let all the ends of the earth revere him.

We have been looking in Psalms at how we can continue to praise God in times of hardship, loneliness, spiritual dryness and with awareness of sin. Sometimes, though, it is the good times that present a challenge. Psalms 65 and 67 praise God for the harvest—the crop is good, God has provided and his people thank him for it. Yet, blessing is always only one step away from self-sufficiency, as God warned his people when they entered the Promised Land: 'You may say to yourself, "My power and the strength of my hands have produced this wealth for me"' (Deuteronomy 8:17, NIV). Often when life is going well and we feel secure, we forget just how dependent on God we are. It is more than just neglecting to thank him for his blessings. When we cease to acknowledge that God is the source of everything we have, two things can happen.

First, we become possessive. We are less inclined to share what we have earned. Our attitude may be, 'I can manage by myself and so should others!' Seeing that ability to manage as a gift from God, however, makes us more inclined to help others who cannot.

Second, we forget that God is Lord of all. The psalmist talks about God's saving power being known among all nations as they praise God for what he has done. If his people do not bear witness to all he does in their lives, the rest of the world will not know his greatness, that his saving power is there for all who call on him.

Reflection

How can my life be a better witness to the blessings that God has given me?

JC

Tuesday 22 November

Psalm 68:1, 4, 24–25, 27 (NIV)

Familiar words

May God arise, may his enemies be scattered; may his foes flee before him... Sing to God, sing praise to his name, extol him who rides on the clouds—his name is the Lord—and rejoice before him... Your procession has come into view, O God, the procession of my God and King into the sanctuary. In front are the singers, after them the musicians; with them are the maidens playing tambourines... There is the little tribe of Benjamin, leading them, there the great throng of Judah's princes, and there the princes of Zebulun and of Naphtali.

The procession for which this psalm was written may have been the return of the Ark to Jerusalem (2 Samuel 6). Afterwards, it was used in the festival of Weeks, when the harvest was gathered in. It speaks of a God who has been with his people through their history, in their family relationships and who is present in their country. He is a God who goes with them on journeys (vv. 1–9) and is with them when they settle down (vv. 16–27). This is the God who they encounter in worship and every aspect of life.

As you read many of the psalms, you may well find that you come across familiar words and phrases. Perhaps you find a tune you know going through your head unbidden, as the words bring to mind hymns and songs. Throughout the history of Christian worship, we have drawn on the psalms for inspiration. This psalm does the same thing as it draws on the words of Deborah's song (Judges 5) and, in its very first verse, reminds the people of the traditional words of Moses in the desert (Numbers 10:35).

It is good to draw on the heritage of the past in worship, especially on the words of scripture. Like regularly reading the Bible in daily study, using the words meaningfully in worship helps to make them part of our lives, deep down in our hearts where God can speak to us. We also have in the psalms a language of praise, as we have seen, that is not just for the good times but also for every area of life.

Reflection
Choose a psalm or part of a psalm to use to worship God today.

JC

A royal wedding

My heart is stirred by a noble theme as I recite my verses for the king; my tongue is the pen of a skilful writer... Your throne, O God, will last for ever and ever; a sceptre of justice will be the sceptre of your kingdom. You love righteousness and hate wickedness; therefore God, your God, has set you above your companions by anointing you with the oil of joy... All glorious is the princess within her chamber; her gown is interwoven with gold. In embroidered garments she is led to the king; her virgin companions follow her and are brought to you.

How was the Bible written? How did the writings of many different individuals become the inspired word of God? Psalm 44 tells us how the writer was inspired by an oral tradition, the stories of his ancestors (44:1). The author of this psalm speaks out of the overflowing of his heart, relating the messages as faithfully as a scribe taking down what is dictated. The result is a wonderfully vivid wedding song and something that over the years has been found to be far more.

It is a very sensual psalm, full of the sounds, scents and sights of a royal wedding. Some may be surprised to find something as 'secular' as a marriage song in a book of worship, but the psalmist sees no discontinuity between the joy of a royal wedding and the worship of God, between the king as God's representative and the reign of God himself as king over all.

Because he sees God in all of life—not keeping the sacred in a compartment away from everyday experience—the psalmist writes words that resonate still with us today. The writer of the letter to the Hebrews picks up verses 6 and 7 as referring to Jesus (Hebrews 1:8–9), who is not only king but also God, whose reign of righteousness will last forever.

What of the bride? The image of the bride is used in several places in the Bible to describe God's relationship with his people (Isaiah 62:5; Jeremiah 31:32; Ephesians 5:31–2; Revelation 19:7). It speaks of love and a lasting, covenant relationship. It is the relationship to which God calls us all.

Prayer

Thank God that he is with us in the whole of life and calls us into relationship with him.

JC

Listening to the psalms

My eyes fail looking for my God. Those who hate me without reason outnumber the hairs of my head; many are my enemies without cause, those who seek to destroy me. I am forced to restore
what I did not steal... for zeal for your house consumes me, and
the insults of those who insult you fall on me... May the table set
before them become a snare; may it become retribution and a trap.
May their eyes be darkened so that they cannot see, and their
backs be bent for ever... May their place be deserted; let there be
no one to dwell in their tents.

In our study of several psalms, we
have seen how the words can be
written by one person in a particular situation, yet used in worship
by many. They were written long
ago, yet we can find in them things
relevant to our own situation
today. Some of them, like yesterday's reading, have also been
understood at another level.
Several were picked up by writers
of the New Testament and applied
to Jesus.

The psalm we are looking at
today is quoted by New Testament
writers more than any other, with
all the verses quoted above and
others being seen as relating to
Jesus and the new situation he
brought about (see, for example,
John 2:17; Acts 1:20; Romans
11:9–10). Indeed, Paul writes that
'whatever was written in former
days was written for our instruction, so that by steadfastness and
by the encouragement of the scrip-

tures we might have hope'
(Romans 15:4, NRSV).

This should not encourage us
to see the Bible as some sort of
code book by means of which we
can work out God's secret message
to us. Indeed, we should be very
wary of taking passages out of context or seeing hidden meanings in
obscure texts. The best way to hear
God's word is in regular, prayerful
reading of the Bible. We should
not miss out the passages that we
may find difficult or uncomfortable, as much of this psalm is, but
instead ask God to help us, by his
Spirit and by the use of resources
such as these notes, to be people
who not only hear his word but
also live it.

Reflection

*What has challenged or encouraged
you in our readings from the
selected psalms?*

JC

PSALM 71:5–6, 9, 17–18 (NIV)

A faith for the whole of life

For you have been my hope, O Sovereign Lord, my confidence since my youth. From my birth I have relied on you; you brought me forth from my mother's womb. I will ever praise you... Do not cast me away when I am old; do not forsake me when my strength is gone... Since my youth, O God, you have taught me, and to this day I declare your marvellous deeds. Even when I am old and grey, do not forsake me, O God, till I declare your power to the next generation, your might to all who are to come.

Unlike the other psalms in Psalms, this one does not have a specific title. It is not for a specific occasion and does not arise out of a particular happening, but takes in the whole of life. God is the God who is there with us throughout our lives. As we have looked at different psalms, we have seen how God is with us whether we are in familiar places or away from home, in good times or hard, when we are close to him and when we stray away. He is with his people but is God of the whole earth. This psalm acknowledges God as the God of our whole lives, from its beginning until its end.

Whether we are young or old, it is never the wrong time to seek God's way or know his blessing in our lives. We should never assume that we—or other people—are too young or too old to be used in God's purposes or to be valuable to him. Stories about how God used people others considered too young (1 Samuel 17:42) or too old (Genesis 17:17) still stand as reminders that we cannot limit God's grace.

Each generation tends to think that wisdom begins and ends with them. Whatever our age, we can thank God that he is with us and remains so all our lives. We can resolve to value the gifts that he has given to those younger and older than us so that we can all learn from each other.

Prayer

Thank God for his different blessings at each stage of life, especially the stage you are at now.

JC

PSALM 72:1–2, 4–5, 7, 17 (NRSV)

The coming king

Give the king your justice, O God, and your righteousness to a king's son. May he judge your people with righteousness, and your poor with justice… May he defend the cause of the poor of the people, give deliverance to the needy, and crush the oppressor. May he live while the sun endures, and as long as the moon, throughout all generations… In his days may righteousness flourish and peace abound, until the moon is no more… May his name endure for ever, his fame continue as long as the sun. May all nations be blessed in him; may they pronounce him happy.

This psalm is headed 'of Solomon' and may have been written by David in anticipation of his son becoming king after him. It tells of a time of transition and hope as the nation moves into new times, with a new ruler. It asks that God will bless the king and give him the gifts he needs and expresses the confidence that it will be so, that God's anointed leader will be the sort of person needed to do the job.

There are echoes in this psalm of a much greater king to come. This is a king who will fulfil God's promise to Abraham not just for the Israelite nation but also for the whole world (v. 7: see Genesis 12:3) and all time (v. 5). It is a king whose reign brings about a time of perfect peace. Note that the Hebrew word 'shalom' means completeness—not just the absence of conflict, but harmony of the whole community in a right relationship with God.

Tomorrow is Advent Sunday, the start of the new year in the Church and a time when we look to the ultimate fulfilment of the vision of this psalm. We also look forward to the time when God's kingdom will be established throughout the world and Christ will come not as the helpless baby of Christmastide but the great king we read about here. Meanwhile, we live in hope and confidence, praying that God will bring about what he has promised and what will surely happen in his time.

Prayer

As we pray, 'Your kingdom come', pray for those who lead us now, that God will give them the gifts and right judgment they need.

JC

Revelation 5—14

Advent is usually swamped by what the media call 'the run up to Christmas'. By now, the Christmas displays are in the shops and carols are being played over the sound systems. Even in church, Advent is truncated by all the carol services, nativity plays and so on. As a result, the traditional Advent themes of final judgment and the second coming of Christ are drowned out by jollification.

Well, not in this year's *New Daylight*! Here we are about to embark on three weeks of readings from one of the most uncompromisingly severe sections of the Bible: Revelation 5—14. In the course of Christian history, they have proved a happy hunting ground for those who favour eccentric exegesis. Some have seen here a detailed road map of the future of the human race. Some have gloried in its awesome pictures of fire, famine, plague and death. Others have concerned themselves with defining more precisely who will be saved from all these calamities (usually the religious group to which they belong) and who will end up in the lake of fire.

Most biblical scholars reject such an approach, seeing Revelation as a coded message to the Church at the time of its writing and, because of divine inspiration, the Church in succeeding ages. It was written at a time when Christians were beginning to experience persecution at the hands of the Roman emperors and fully expected more to follow. Had God a message for his people in these dark and terrible times? If so, what was it?

Revelation—*apocalypses* in the Greek—means an 'unfolding of meaning'. This style of writing, common enough in the ancient world, requires interpretation or, in more ordinary language, decoding. We are given clues as to what the code is, but it is up to the reader to apply them. In this way, a strong message can be conveyed with a minimum of offence.

The message of Revelation is couched in a succession of vivid images and visions. Understanding them lies as much in our imagination as our reason, but when we use both we shall find—as many generations of Christians have done—that here is a message for the darkest times. At the heart of eternity and on the throne of the universe sit two figures of wonderful reassurance: the Lord God and the Lamb, who 'takes away the sin of the world' (John 1:29).

David Winter

REVELATION 5:6–8 (NRSV)

The power of the Lamb

Then I saw between the throne and the four living creatures and among the elders a Lamb standing as if it had been slaughtered, having seven horns and seven eyes, which are the seven spirits of God sent out into all the earth. He went and took the scroll from the right hand of the one who was seated on the throne. When he had taken the scroll, the four living creatures and the twenty-four elders fell before the Lamb, each holding a harp and golden bowls full of incense, which are the prayers of the saints.

The one seated on the throne in this vision is 'our Lord and God' (4:11) and in his right hand there is a scroll covered with writing—obviously an important message. The scroll is sealed, however, and the 'mighty angel' (5:2) fears that there is no one worthy to open it. The human observer of this vision—distressed that its profound truths might never be revealed—is reassured that 'The Lion of the tribe of Judah' (v. 5) has conquered and is able to break the seals.

When Jacob blessed his sons, he called Judah a 'lion's whelp' (Genesis 49:9), so, over the centuries, the 'Lion of Judah' became a title of the Messiah, who was to come from the tribe of Judah. Here we learn that the 'Lion' is also a 'Lamb'—an amazing paradox! Not only that, but he is a Lamb 'standing as if it had been slaughtered'—although it was alive, it bore the awful marks of the slaughterhouse on its neck.

The Lamb—obviously Jesus—also has seven horns and seven eyes, which are 'the seven spirits of God sent out into all the earth'. The Spirit of God is therefore perfectly present in Jesus—seven being the number of completeness.

Presumably, the message of this vision is that the great hidden truths of time and eternity written on God's scroll can only be ours through the death of the 'Lamb of God' and the presence of God's Spirit. At this revelation, the four living creatures ('four' in Revelation speaks of creation) and the twenty-four elders fall before the Lamb in adoration.

Sunday reflection

The cross of Jesus unfolds the meaning of our existence and the profoundest truth about God's purposes. The seal on the scroll can be broken!

DW

The new song

They [The four living creatures and twenty-four elders] sing a new song: 'You are worthy to take the scroll and to open its seals, for you were slaughtered and by your blood you ransomed for God saints from every tribe and language and people and nation; you have made them to be a kingdom and priests serving our God, and they will reign on earth.' Then I looked, and I heard the voice of many angels surrounding the throne and the living creatures and the elders; they numbered myriads of myriads and thousands of thousands, singing with full voice, 'Worthy is the Lamb that was slaughtered to receive power and wealth and wisdom and might and honour and glory and blessing!'

New songs aren't always popular, as any minister knows, but if you never sing any new songs, there won't be any old ones to sing in 100 years' time! The 'old song' is often about a comfortable and cosy religion—as familiar as a favourite pair of slippers. The 'new song' can speak of a new insight into the timeless truth of God. Certainly, the new song of the saints in heaven in this vision expressed the wonder of the new revelation: the Lion/Lamb, Jesus, was able to open the book of the mystery of God's purposes. At last, the full truth of our redemption could be revealed.

What gave the Lamb this authority? The answer is in the song: 'for you were slaughtered and by your blood you ransomed for God saints from every tribe and language and people and nation' (v. 9). It was through his death on the cross that

freedom was secured—not simply for the people of the old covenant, but for those from every nation and culture on Earth. This new freedom is available to all, without fear or favour. The ransomed people would now be the new kingdom of priests to serve God, not so much replacing the old order as incorporating it into the new one.

So, the 'slaughtered Lamb' is worthy of every honour God can bestow—power, wealth, wisdom and might, honour, glory and blessing. He might look like a victim, but in truth he is the victor. No wonder the elders fell down and worshipped (v. 14)!

Reflection

Real victory, true power, comes through the self-sacrificing love of the cross.

DW

The deadly horsemen

Then I saw the Lamb open one of the seven seals, and I heard one of the four living creatures call out, as with a voice of thunder, 'Come!' I looked, and there was a white horse! Its rider had a bow; a crown was given to him, and he came out conquering and to conquer. When he opened the second seal, I heard the second living creature call out, 'Come!' And out came another horse, bright red; its rider was permitted to take peace from the earth, so that people would slaughter one another; and he was given a great sword.

These are the first two of the 'horsemen of the Apocalypse', each signifying one of the terrifying perils that can be experienced on earth. The first horse represents conquest—victory by the sword. The people who first heard these prophecies would have known well the power of Rome, achieved by the might and discipline of its legions. Sometimes that power was used well—there were good dictators as well as bad ones. Sometimes it was used brutally, as the Church experienced under Nero.

The second horseman represents war. Of all the plagues that have afflicted humanity, this is probably the most devastating and certainly the most obviously self-inflicted. It is disconcerting to read that the rider was 'permitted to take peace from the earth, so that people would slaughter one another' (v. 4), as though wars occur with divine permission. In fact, the 'permission' here is the terrifying gift of moral autonomy, or 'free will'. God has given to his self-conscious human creatures the fearful right to do wrong. It is a 'right' that we have exploited to the full.

The appearance of each of the four horsemen is preceded by a call from one of the 'living creatures' to 'Come!' This is not an invitation to the horsemen, but to the Lord Jesus—'Come, Lord Jesus!', which is another recurrent theme in this book. Only then will a battered, sin-strewn planet and its inhabitants find true peace, health and security.

Reflection

This chapter ends with people hiding from 'the wrath of the Lamb'—another amazing paradox. Kings of the earth, magnates and generals (v. 15) will flee before God's judgment. The earth may suffer for a time, but justice will be done.

DW

The great multitude

'Do not damage the earth or the sea or the trees, until we have marked the servants of our God with a seal on their foreheads.' And I heard the number of those who were sealed, 144,000, sealed out of every tribe of the people of Israel... After this I looked, and there was a great multitude that no one could count, from every nation, from all tribes and peoples and languages, standing before the throne and before the Lamb, robed in white, with palm branches in their hands.

Between chapters 6 and 16 of Revelation there are three series of seven judgments—seven seals, seven trumpets and seven bowls. Each contains four judgments followed by another three—the distinction perhaps being between natural disasters and divine judgments. The first two sets of seven also contain what might be called 'inspirational intervals', revealing the splendour and joy of the saints in heaven. This passage is part of one of those interludes.

It hardly needs saying, but the word 'saint' in the New Testament does not exclusively refer to someone who has been canonized by the Church. The 'saints' of God are those who have been saved by Christ and so made holy. 'Saint' simply means 'holy' (from the Latin word *sanctus*), one who is counted holy in the sight of God. Martyrdom, in the early centuries of the Church's life, was the ultimate test of sainthood, but not all the saints were martyrs.

In this amazing vision, John sees the great multitude of those who had been marked with a 'seal' on their foreheads (7:3). This 'sealing' probably refers to the ancient practice of using chrism to make a mark (probably of the cross) on the foreheads of candidates for baptism. Certainly, the continuing practice tends to look back to this scene in Revelation. The seal was like the brand with which owners marked their slaves: he belongs to me. Christians proudly wear the seal, the brand of Christ: 'I belong to him'.

In the vision, 144,000 from the tribes of Israel were thus sealed (twelve times twelve: a number of completeness), but from the 'nations' it was simply a 'great multitude that no one could count', robed in the white robe of baptism.

Reflection

To whom do I belong?
Whom do I serve?

DW

REVELATION 7:13–17 (NRSV)

The Shepherd-Lamb

Then one of the elders addressed me, saying, 'Who are these, robed in white, and where have they come from?' I said to him, 'Sir, you are the one that knows.' Then he said to me, 'These are they who have come out of the great ordeal; they have washed their robes and made them white in the blood of the Lamb. For this reason they are before the throne of God, and worship him day and night within his temple, and the one who is seated on the throne will shelter them. They will hunger no more, and thirst no more; the sun will not strike them, nor any scorching heat; for the Lamb at the centre of the throne will be their shepherd, and he will guide them to springs of the water of life, and God will wipe away every tear from their eyes.'

The spectator is very much part of the vision, as one of the 'elders' asks him the identity of the vast throng clad in white. Strangely, the dialogue reveals that he knew the answer all along—they are those who have 'come out of the great ordeal' (v. 14). This may be the ordeal of martyrdom or living through the time of testing of which Jesus spoke (Mark 13:19). Either way, they are Christians who have triumphed in the cosmic battle of faith, which has often been real and bloody for a persecuted Church.

It is not their courage nor their fortitude that has saved them, however, but the 'blood of the Lamb'—the self-sacrificial love of Calvary. It is that sacrifice alone that enables them (as it will enable us) to stand in the heavenly temple and serve God. Here, the disasters and plagues are no more. Instead, the Lamb seated on the throne will be their 'shepherd'. We have had the 'wrath of the Lamb' and here we have a Lamb who is also a shepherd! He died for them and now leads them to springs of living water, where God himself will wipe away their tears.

Reflection

Heaven is not a place of passive adoration, but an environment of active service. That is the meaning of the word translated as 'worship' here—it means offering our lives, our gifts and our bodies in service to the living God.

DW

The prayers of the saints

When the Lamb opened the seventh seal, there was silence in heaven for about half an hour. And I saw the seven angels who stand before God, and seven trumpets were given to them. Another angel with a golden censer came and stood at the altar; he was given a great quantity of incense to offer with the prayers of all the saints on the golden altar that is before the throne. And the smoke of the incense, with the prayers of the saints, rose before God from the hand of the angel. Then the angel took the censer and filled it with fire from the altar and threw it on the earth; and there were peals of thunder, rumblings, flashes of lightning, and an earthquake.

As the last seal is opened, heaven falls silent. In fact, we aren't told its contents until after the seven angels had blown their trumpets and the consequent disasters have occurred. This is not a mistake by the author, but seems intended to assure the reader that these events are simultaneous. Revelation is not giving us an orderly picture of events to come, but describing the meaning of events that are going on somewhere all the while.

At any rate, there is silence before there is prayer. Someone has suggested that in the silence God listens before we speak—and if we are wise, before we speak we shall listen, too. Prayer is not so much our initiative as a response to the loving purpose of God. That's why the perfect prayer is always 'Your will, not mine, O Lord'.

The imagery of the next few verses beautifully indicates the deepest truth about prayer. It ascends like incense to the throne of God from the altar of sacrifice. Prayer is not routine, light or easy but the costly offering of ourselves to the fulfilment of God's purposes. Here it would seem that the prayers were for vindication under suffering and persecution—a cry from the heart for God to act on behalf of his stricken people.

The divine response is immediate. The angel hurls the censer filled with the incense of the prayers on the earth—and verse 5 describes the results!

Reflection

Silently surrendered to the will of God, we utter the deep prayers of our hearts.

DW

The destroyer

They have as king over them the angel of the bottomless pit; his name in Hebrew is Abaddon and in Greek he is called Apollyon. The first woe has passed. There are still two woes to come.

The 'they' in the first sentence is the locusts, the arrival of which, in vast numbers, signifies the first 'woe' at the sounding of the fifth trumpet (vv. 3–10). I have chosen it to represent the rest of the woes simply because plagues of locusts have a long biblical tradition and understanding that fact may help us to appreciate what these hideous plagues are meant to convey to the reader.

Clearly these particular locusts are not insects in the ordinary meaning of the word. They come from the 'bottomless pit' (v. 2), stimulated into action by a falling star—presumably a satanic angel. The abyss is the same word (in Greek) as the 'formless void' of Genesis 1:2—a place of meaninglessness and emptiness. We also have hordes of locusts as one of the plagues of Egypt (Exodus 10:12–15) and in the prophet Joel's writings, where God's judgment is likened to an army of locusts (Joel 1:4). In Revelation, more clearly than elsewhere, the locusts are themselves seen as demonic—they attack humans, yet do not harm the grass or green growth (the usual diet of the locust). They are instruments of pain, yet not of death. They are not able to harm those who 'have the seal of God on their foreheads' (v. 4).

What does it all mean? The passage quoted above seems to be the clue. The 'king of the locusts' has a name: Abaddon or Apollyon. Both mean much the same thing—'destruction' and 'destroyer', respectively. Evil, in other words, is ultimately purposeless. It makes nothing of value and destroys what is good. Yet, even this most horrific picture of evil on the rampage is within the controlling purpose of God. It will be judged, and destruction itself will eventually be destroyed. It is a sombre message, but who can doubt its relevance, looking at the world we live in?

Reflection

Revelation shows us God's two counters to the reign of unfettered evil. One is the Lamb on the throne; the other is the judge of all the Earth. They are the same person!

DW

No repentance

The rest of humankind, who were not killed by these plagues, did not repent of the works of their hands or give up worshipping demons and idols of gold and silver and bronze and stone and wood, which cannot see or hear or walk. And they did not repent of their murders or their sorceries or their fornication or their thefts.

Relentlessly, the vision of evil moves on. Now we have the army of evil—200 million was the number John heard (v. 16). It is an unstoppable cavalry, riding on mystical horses with lions' heads and fire, smoke and sulphur coming out of their mouths (v. 17). Whatever else, we are not meant to take this literally. Here is the ultimate picture of mass destruction, which, in the vision, accounted for a third of the world's population (v. 18).

One might have supposed that, faced with this appalling disaster, people would have turned to God and repented. In fact, nothing of the sort happened. Despite the plagues, suffering, bloodshed and horror, they 'did not repent' or 'give up worshipping demons and idols of gold and silver and bronze and stone and wood' (vv. 20–21). They didn't even repent of their more everyday sins—theft, murder and sexual promiscuity.

This vision is like an extended documentary on 'the wages of sin is death' (Romans 6:23). A world that lives without God is always in peril of dying without him, too, and there is no fate more abject than that. Evil and destruction, the vision tells us, are much the same thing. However appealing sin may seem, its final effect is to destroy people, families, communities, even nations and empires. It is not that God is a cruel or relentless judge, but that evil brings about its own judgment. It is a kind of moral suicide.

Sunday reflection

There are two sombre aspects of this picture of judgment. The first is that it came in response to the prayers of the saints—the 'golden altar before God' in verse 14 is the altar of offered prayer. The second is that its time was preordained (v. 15). God's judgment may be long delayed, but, if it is, it is out of mercy, not weakness. That seems a good subject of meditation for the second Sunday in Advent.

DW

The bittersweet message

And I saw another mighty angel coming down from heaven… He held a little scroll open in his hand… So I went to the angel and told him to give me the little scroll; and he said to me, 'Take it, and eat; it will be bitter to your stomach, but sweet as honey in your mouth.' So I took the little scroll from the hand of the angel and ate it; it was sweet as honey in my mouth, but when I had eaten it, my stomach was made bitter. Then they said to me, 'You must prophesy again about many peoples and nations and languages and kings.'

Now John becomes a participant in the drama. A 'mighty angel' (v. 1) hands him a little scroll and a voice from heaven directs him to eat it (v. 8). This is rather like the experience of the prophet Ezekiel, who was also told to take a scroll and eat it (Ezekiel 3:2) and then prophesy to the people in captivity. Here, when the scroll has been consumed, John receives a similar authorization to prophesy (v. 11).

Ezekiel's scroll was sweet to the taste, but John's was both sweet and bitter—sweet in his mouth but bitter in his stomach. This seems to be a dramatic way of saying that its message would be sweet for some and bitter for others.

What is this message? We are told that the time had come for the 'mystery of God' to be fulfilled, 'as he announced to his servants the prophets' (v. 7). All through the New Testament, and especially in the letters of Paul, there is mention of this 'mystery'—a mystery finally made known through the gospel of Jesus. Paul claimed that he had been sent by God's commission to make known 'the mystery that has been hidden throughout the ages… but has now been revealed to his saints'. For Paul, the 'riches of the glory' of this mystery, is simply this: 'Christ in [or among] you, the hope of glory' (see Colossians 1:25–27). The mystery, in other words, is God's great saving purpose for the world, hidden for long ages but revealed through Jesus and his Church.

Reflection

The message of the Gospels is always sweet and bitter. After all, the same Jesus is both the world's Saviour and its Judge.

DW

Promise of better things

Then the seventh angel blew his trumpet, and there were loud voices in heaven, saying, 'The kingdom of the world has become the kingdom of our Lord and of his Messiah, and he will reign for ever and ever.' Then the 24 elders who sit on their thrones before God fell on their faces and worshipped God, singing, 'We give you thanks, Lord God Almighty, who are and who were, for you have taken your great power and begun to reign. The nations raged, but your wrath has come, and the time for judging the dead, for rewarding your servants, the prophets and saints and all who fear your name, both small and great, and for destroying those who destroy the earth.'

'The time has come'—that is the core message of this passage: the time both of God's judgment and his salvation. Although in the course of Revelation more evil will be described, this passage signals the eventual victory of God. What follows is a kind of mopping-up operation. Hostilities are not over, but the final result of the conflict is now assured.

Voices from heaven set the scene of victory in words many of us know from Handel's *Messiah*: 'The kingdom of this world has become the kingdom of our Lord and of his Christ (Messiah)'. This is the language of the 'prophetic future'—events that are part of God's plans but not yet realized. The vision sees God as already present among his people in a new way. The elders sing praise to the Lord God Almighty 'who are and who were' —no mention here of 'and are to come', because he has come. He is now among his people; he has gathered them to himself.

This moment of triumph has two consequences: the final destruction of evil and the rewarding of 'God's servants, the prophets and saints' and—enlarging the horizons of salvation—'all who fear your name' (v. 18). The two processes will be parallel. As we shall see, the heart of evil is not so much human sinfulness as demonic destructiveness. Good cannot reign until evil has been destroyed. What remains is the final overthrow of these malign influences in God's creation and their consignment to 'the lake of fire' (20:15).

Reflection

*We sing 'Our God reigns'—
and he will!*

DW

The child saviour

A great portent appeared in heaven: a woman clothed with the sun, with the moon under her feet, and on her head a crown of twelve stars. She was pregnant and was crying out in birth pangs... Then another portent appeared in heaven: a great red dragon, with seven heads and ten horns, and seven diadems on his heads... Then the dragon stood before the woman who was about to bear a child, so that he might devour her child as soon as it was born. And she gave birth to a son, a male child, who is to rule all the nations with a rod of iron. But her child was snatched away and taken to God and to his throne; and the woman fled into the wilderness, where she has a place prepared by God.

It's not hard for the Christian reader to see in this strange vision the story of Jesus. The woman is presumably Israel, the people of God (the twelve stars standing for the twelve tribes and in the new dispensation the twelve apostles). From that woman, as was foretold to Eve, would come the offspring that would strike the head of the evil serpent (Genesis 3:15). Many Christians have also seen here a picture of Mary, the mother of Jesus, which is a reasonable inference, provided we see her as representative of the whole of God's people, both Israel and the Church.

The child is clearly Jesus, who would 'rule all the nations with a rod of iron' (v. 5). John has already put these words into the mouth of Christ (Revelation 2:27) and will do so again in 19:15, and in 19:13 he is identified as the 'Word of God'. Although the dragon is powerful, the child is snatched from his clutches and taken to God and his throne—language encompassing both the resurrection and ascension. The people of God are taken to a desert place of safety prepared by God.

What Revelation is now spelling out is the undercover story of the machinations of demonic evil and the battle that eventually led to the outcome that the 'kingdom of the world has become the kingdom of our Lord and of his Messiah' (11:15).

Reflection

Our salvation was not lightly won, nor is life 'in the desert' necessarily comfortable!

DW

War in heaven

And war broke out in heaven; Michael and his angels fought against the dragon. The dragon and his angels fought back, but they were defeated, and there was no longer any place for them in heaven. The great dragon was thrown down, that ancient serpent, who is called the Devil and Satan, the deceiver of the whole world—he was thrown down to the earth, and his angels were thrown down with him. Then I heard a loud voice in heaven, proclaiming, 'Now have come the salvation and the power and the kingdom of our God and the authority of his Messiah, for the accuser of our comrades has been thrown down, who accuses them day and night before our God.'

This is a strange passage to modern ears, but not quite so strange if we set it in the context of the story of the woman, dragon and child in yesterday's passage. At the end of it, the child—Jesus—had returned to the throne of God, from whence he would rule or, literally, 'shepherd' all the nations. The victory over death and sin had been won and John's first readers and hearers would have had no doubt about the heart of that victory: the death and resurrection of Jesus.

Now, in this story of 'war in heaven', we are shown that the victory of Christ was not simply in the earthly realm and does not only affect God's human creatures. It was also a victory in the spiritual realm of heaven (not, here, the final place of glory for the saints, but the world beyond this world). In that celestial sphere, the true cosmic drama was worked out. The old enemy, Satan (literally, the 'adversary'), is expelled and the final triumph of God and goodness can be celebrated. The conquest, we notice, is Christ's, within the purposes of God (v. 10), not that of Michael and his angels, however mighty they are. When the story of the woman is resumed at verse 13, we shall see that there are still those mopping-up operations to be concluded, but the final triumph of God is assured.

Reflection

Satan is the 'accuser' of the Christians before God; Jesus is the 'excuser' of them before the same throne. 'Guilty', screams Satan. 'Forgiven', says our Saviour.

DW

Those who conquer

'But they have conquered him [the accuser] by the blood of the Lamb and by the word of their testimony, for they did not cling to life even in the face of death. Rejoice then, you heavens and those who dwell in them! But woe to the earth and the sea, for the devil has come down to you with great wrath, because he knows that his time is short!'

Here the two kingdoms—Earth and heaven—are made clear. In heaven, the victory of the Lamb is celebrated, but on earth the conquered enemy is still active, though his days are numbered. The 'they' in the first sentence is the saints—those whom Satan has falsely accused and tried to defeat. The weapons of conquests are not the swords of Michael and his angels, but 'the blood of the Lamb' (v. 11) and their own faithfulness to him, even in the face of death.

Some readers of the Bible are somewhat put off by references to the blood of Christ and especially any notion of being 'washed' in it. They are not just being squeamish; they find the imagery unhelpful, even grotesque. We need to see this as the language of sacrifice, however. The Lamb would have been a familiar image of sacrifice to Jewish readers and hearers, from the earliest days of the patriarchs to the time of Jesus. After all, Israel was delivered from slavery in Egypt by means of the sacrifice of many Passover lambs. The 'blood of Christ' is simply shorthand for the whole idea of the self-sacrificing love of Jesus, who gave himself for us on the cross.

The triumph celebrated by the saints in heaven is precisely that victory—the victory of love over hatred, of forgiveness over retribution. In the cross, evil has been defeated by love. Satan knows this, but he is still able—in his death throes, as it were—to inflict evil and woe on the earth. Nevertheless, 'his time is short' (v. 12). God's victory is assured.

Reflection

'Your kingdom come, your will be done on Earth, as it is in heaven'. Every time we pray those words, we acknowledge that there are two kingdoms, but we long that they may become 'the kingdom of our Lord and of his Messiah' (Revelation 11:15).

DW

The beast and his power

The beast was given a mouth uttering haughty and blasphemous words, and it was allowed to exercise authority for 42 months. It opened its mouth to utter blasphemies against God, blaspheming his name and his dwelling, that is, those who dwell in heaven. Also it was allowed to make war on the saints and to conquer them. It was given authority over every tribe and people and language and nation, and all the inhabitants of the earth will worship it, everyone whose name has not been written from the foundation of the world in the book of life of the Lamb that was slaughtered.

We now learn that the dragon—Satan—has an ally—a mysterious beast with ten horns and seven heads (like the dragon) and the predatory tastes of a leopard, lion and bear. Eventually, his identity will be disclosed, but 'let anyone who has an ear listen' (v. 9)—think carefully and you may well work out the answer.

We learn two terrible things about the beast. The first is that it had universal sway over the nations. 'It was given authority'—presumably by God—'over every tribe and people and language and nation' (v. 7). Not only that, but their entire populations would worship it, except for those who belonged to the Lamb and whose names were written in his book. (The alternative reading in the NRSV footnote follows the Greek text more closely—it was the Lamb who was slain 'from the foundation of the world', v. 8.)

The other terrible thing about the beast is its enmity towards the Church ('his [God's] name and his dwelling', v. 6). It waged war on the Christians and conquered them. Evil always longs to control people and force them to follow its own ways and it has always hated those who seek to follow God's standards of peace and justice. Again, we are reminded, however, that the beast's power is limited. It has a sell-by date stamped on it by God—it has authority for just '42 months'!

Reflection

We should not be surprised that evil manifests itself by seeking to enslave people and not simply by force of arms but also by economic and commercial means. Nor should the Church expect to be approved of by the forces of evil—the two are on a moral collision course.

DW

REVELATION 13:11–18 (NRSV, ABRIDGED)

Its name revealed

Then I saw another beast that rose out of the earth; it had two horns like a lamb and it spoke like a dragon. It exercises all the authority of the first beast on its behalf, and it makes the earth and its inhabitants worship the first beast... Also it causes all, both small and great, both rich and poor, both free and slave, to be marked on the right hand or the forehead, so that no one can buy or sell who does not have the mark, that is, the name of the beast or the number of its name. This calls for wisdom: let anyone with understanding calculate the number of the beast, for it is the number of a person. Its number is 666.

Let's start with the number of this second beast—666. John's first hearers probably had little difficulty in decoding the number, which is based on the substitution of numerical values for alphabetical letters. The Greek word for 'beast', put into Hebrew letters and then their number equivalents is 666, as is the Greek form of 'Nero Caesar'.

They might well have identified the second beast already, because there are many clues here pointing (for people of the time) to the Roman Empire and its emperors. The Emperor claimed divine status and required of his subjects the equivalent of divine worship. Christians who would not do this (by burning incense on the imperial altars) were disqualified from business and public life—and sometimes worse (see v. 17). Just as Christians were seen in this visionary language as bearing on their foreheads the baptismal mark of Christ, so the followers of the Emperor were marked with the number of the beast.

The vision gives nothing less than satanic status to the Emperor and his empire—they are serving the 'first beast' (v. 12) and promoting worship of him. To the Christians of the first century, it must sometimes have seemed that it was not the Lamb but the beast who was on the throne of the universe.

Sunday reflection

It is very easy to fall for the false glamour of worldly power, even when it manifests itself in naked injustice and oppression. Advent should remind us that, in the end, true power and holy justice belong only to God.

DW

REVELATION 14:1–3 (NRSV)

The new song

Then I looked, and there was the Lamb, standing on Mount Zion! And with him were 144,000 who had his name and his Father's name written on their foreheads. And I heard a voice from heaven like the sound of many waters and like the sound of loud thunder; the voice I heard was like the sound of harpists playing on their harps, and they sing a new song before the throne and before the four living creatures and before the elders.

It may indeed have seemed to John's first hearers that it was the beast and not the Lamb who was on the throne, but the very next vision corrects the impression dramatically. He 'looked' and there was the Lamb, 'standing on Mount Zion' (v. 1), the heavenly Jerusalem —and surrounded by a might army of combatants! Again, they number 144,000—a number of completeness, yet these are merely the 'first fruits' of that vast multitude 'that no one could count', which will one day surround the heavenly throne (see verse 4 and compare with 7:9). They do not bear the mark of the beast on their foreheads, but instead the names of the Lamb and his Father.

Then, accompanied by angelic harpists, they sang 'a new song' (v. 3). What might this have been and why was it 'new'? (We've already had one 'new song' in chapter 5.) Surely this one is new because the people of the new covenant now have, through Christ, a new vision of the Father and his purposes. It is a song of truth newly revealed and newly understood—that the evil and corruption of the world, as typified by the beast and his accomplice, have already been defeated in the cross of Christ. This vast heavenly army stands ready to confront evil in the world and overcome it in his name. The purposes of God are not yet complete, but now, at this moment, there stands the Church of Jesus— some in heaven, some on earth— charged to sing a new song, witness to a new truth and overcome the old order with the weaponry of love and self-sacrifice.

Reflection

To sing the new song, one needs a new heart—one that has been redeemed from the corrupt values of the old world order.

DW

REVELATION 14:4–7 (NRSV)

The army and the angel

It is these who have not defiled themselves with women, for they are virgins; these follow the Lamb wherever he goes. They have been redeemed from humankind as first fruits for God and the Lamb, and in their mouth no lie was found; they are blameless. Then I saw another angel flying in mid-heaven, with an eternal gospel to proclaim to those who live on the earth—to every nation and tribe and language and people. He said in a loud voice, 'Fear God and give him glory, for the hour of his judgment has come; and worship him who made heaven and earth, the sea and the springs of water.'

The first sentence here seems quite baffling. Why the reference to women and why are the 144,000 all virgins? The answer lies in the identification of this group of people as an 'army', called by God to counter and then defeat the beast and his empire. First-century armies were entirely male, of course, and, under Mosaic Law, soldiers on active service had to abstain from sex, even with their own wives (hence Uriah's refusal to sleep with Bathsheba, 2 Samuel 11:11). This heavenly army of the redeemed, in other words, is on active service. It has battles to fight and enemies to conquer. This is the Church militant, in the old language, not yet the Church at rest.

These people (men and women, one assumes) are followers of the Lamb 'wherever he goes' (v. 4) and tellers of the truth whatever it costs them. Once that vision had been seen and understood, another appeared—an angel flying in mid-sky, bearing an 'eternal gospel' (v. 6), which was to be proclaimed to all who live on the Earth, 'every nation, tribe, language and people'. The angel personifies the real task of the heavenly army. Their chief weapon to defeat the world's evil is this 'eternal gospel'—good news with eternal consequences. In proclaiming it, they will declare two solemn truths: the hour of God's judgment has arrived but also the hour of the gospel of Christ. This was good news with serious consequences. It always is!

Reflection

Singers of the song, tellers of the truth, followers of the Lamb—this might serve as an excellent rule of life for all Christians. How would we measure up to its standards?

DW

Babylon is fallen!

Then another angel, a second, followed, saying, 'Fallen, fallen is Babylon the great! She has made all nations drink of the wine of the wrath of her fornication... There is no rest day or night for those who worship the beast and its image and for anyone who receives the mark of its name.'

There can be little doubt that for John and his hearers, 'Babylon the great' was imperial Rome. After all, by his day, Babylon was no longer a world power, but she stood in Jewish thought for the powerful oppressor, the one who had taken Israel captive. Now the great Roman empire was doing the same to the 'new Israel'—persecuting the followers of Christ, trying to compel them to acts of sacrilege or blasphemy.

Babylon, though, we are told, will fall and its fall will be catastrophic. The judgment is terrible—read the omitted verses to see its full horror. It is important to stress, however, that the vision does not depict Rome simply as a misguided ruler of nations. After all, Rome did many good things, too. Here, there is a deeper evil at work, something satanic about what has been happening. That would certainly have been how the Roman Christians felt during the first waves of persecution. They had offended no moral or social codes—by general admission, they were law-abiding, honest and loyal citizens. Their one offence was that they believed that there was a higher authority than the Emperor, whom they could not and would not worship as divine. For that they were persecuted and for that persecution, among other things, the empire itself fell under God's judgment.

This is not the judgment of what we might call 'ordinary' human sins and failings, but of what Paul calls the 'cosmic powers of this present darkness', 'the spiritual forces of evil in the heavenly places' (Ephesians 6:12). These enemies of God are not 'blood and flesh', he tells us, but rulers and authorities of a far more sinister kind. Until they are rooted out and destroyed, the world will never be the kingdom of God.

Reflection

'There is no rest... for those who worship the beast' (Revelation 14:11)—one of the penalties of sin, which signals the end of inner peace and the coming of the tortured conscience.

DW

The call to endurance

Here is a call for the endurance of the saints, those who keep the commandments of God and hold fast to the faith of Jesus. And I heard a voice from heaven saying, 'Write this: Blessed are the dead who from now on die in the Lord.' 'Yes,' says the Spirit, 'they will rest from their labours, for their deeds follow them.'

Jesus, speaking of the coming time of testing for his followers, said, 'Anyone who endures to the end will be saved' (Matthew 24:13). Now, in this vision of the Church under persecution, there is a call for just such endurance. It's not a Christian virtue much talked about in Western churches, where love, justice, peace and joy are more evidently sought, yet it remains a quality of discipleship required of many in the face of ridicule, discrimination and, at times, physical attack.

The one who practises endurance has, according to the *Oxford Dictionary*, an 'ability to withstand prolonged strain'. Those who can't 'endure' get going when the going gets tough. For the Christians of the late first century, it was certainly tough and looked likely to get even tougher, yet the record shows that thousands on thousands of Christians 'endured', even to death, and by their witness the Roman empire eventually fell to the gentle rule of Christ.

Earlier in John's vision, the risen Jesus promised the Christians at Smyrna (where the great bishop Polycarp was martyred in the second century) that if they were 'faithful until death', he would give them the 'crown of life' (2:10). Here, those who from now on die 'in the Lord'—that is, the Christian dead—are told that they will be blessed and find the rest the evil are eternally denied (see v. 11). The record of their deeds will follow them to heaven and earn them a place among the ranks of the martyr saints.

We are told the key marks of such endurance: keeping the commandments of God and holding fast to the faith of (or their faith in) Jesus. Faced with lesser trials, or at least less brutal ones, the recipe for true Christian discipleship remains the same.

Reflection

When illness, circumstances, disappointment or despair threaten our faith, may God give us the grace of endurance so that we can be faithful to the end.

DW

The final harvest

Then I looked, and there was a white cloud, and seated on the cloud was one like the Son of Man, with a golden crown on his head, and a sharp sickle in his hand! Another angel came out of the temple, calling with a loud voice to the one who sat on the cloud, 'Use your sickle and reap, for the hour to reap has come, because the harvest of the earth is fully ripe.' So the one who sat on the cloud swung his sickle over the earth, and the earth was reaped.

This is the first of two harvests—highly significant events in biblical times. This one is obviously of grain and it is gathered by Jesus himself. We may therefore assume, from his own parables and teaching, that this is the harvest of those who are to be gathered into the heavenly barns—the good fruit of the kingdom. It is important that the angel, the messenger of God the Father, tells Jesus, the Son, the hour when the reaping is to commence. This is consistent with the teaching of Jesus himself, which is that even he did not know the time of the end, only his Father did. All the more surprising, then, that so many—including Jehovah's Witnesses in our days—have professed to find in these pages a timetable for the end that even Jesus did not know!

At any rate, the harvest is now ripe, the fields are ready to be harvested and, at the appointed time, the Saviour of the world becomes its judge, gathering in his flock from every corner of the earth—people of every tribe, race, language and colour. It is a picture of joy and fulfilment, as is every good harvest. At last, the fruit of the Saviour's painful cross and the costly witness of the martyrs and saints can be gathered in. God's purpose in sending his Son to be the Saviour of the world has been completed.

That is, we might say, the satisfying part of the reaping done. What remains is a second harvest, as we shall see, and that is altogether grimmer.

Reflection

In the story of Jesus, the good seed and the weeds were allowed to grow together (Matthew 13:30), but now the moment has come to separate them.

DW

Judgment at last

Then another angel came out of the temple in heaven, and he too had a sharp sickle. Then another angel came out from the altar, the angel who has authority over fire, and he called with a loud voice to him who had the sharp sickle, 'Use your sharp sickle and gather the clusters of the vine of the earth, for its grapes are ripe.' So the angel swung his sickle over the earth and gathered the vintage of the earth, and he threw it into the great wine press of the wrath of God.

Here is the second harvest—not of the good wheat, but the grapes of evil. The image echoes the language of the prophet Joel (3:13): 'Put in the sickle, for the harvest is ripe… The vats overflow, for their wickedness is great'. We are now witnessing a picture of the final gathering in of all that has spoilt God's creation. The angel's sickle swings and the grapes of wrath are brought into the vats to be trodden, significantly, 'outside the city' (v. 20)—the place of separation, where death sentences were carried out (as happened, of course, to Jesus).

Our readings from Revelation end with two harvests, though if you read on you will see that the final judgment of God has not happened yet. The visions set before us an awesome choice: whose side are we on, God's or his dread adversary?

When Revelation talks of evil, it is not speaking of the ordinary failures of human behaviour that constantly trip us up. This is not the judgment of the one who missed Communion last Sunday or told a 'white lie'. This is evil on a cosmic scale, the rebellion of spirits and humans against the just and loving purposes of God. To leave it unjudged would mean that God is a morally weak ruler, unable or unwilling to do what is right. The final chapters of Revelation show us how, at last, all evil will be rooted out, so that the old earth may become the new heaven and its people the true citizens of God's kingdom.

Reflection

Sometimes it is not enough simply to avoid evil, it must be fought actively. There are no neutrals in the final battle and only one winner— the Lord God, omnipotent.

DW

Celebrating Christmas

Celebration is a common human phenomenon. Everyone finds expressions for celebration, though the causes of our celebrations will vary from continent to continent and culture to culture. So, what does it mean to celebrate?

Celebrating is a group activity, and requires a focus or cause. It may be an occasional event, or annual routine. It might be a national sporting achievement or a wedding anniversary. At the heart of all these celebrations is something of special significance to people. There are also events of wider significance, such as a national victory over an enemy or an amazing achievement, such as people reaching the moon.

In celebrating, emotions are released and shared, but they are also multiplied and amplified. Celebrating is a creative experience, reminding us that people are not isolated islands. We need one another to expand our awareness and joy. While celebrations need a personal element to be truly successful, they need a community dimension as well.

Celebrating is also ritualized—for birthdays, for example, in many countries there will be a special cake with a number of candles equating to the person's age. This ritualizing process becomes more prominent the more nationally and the more routinely the celebration occurs. The fun and excitement can also be increased by organizing events on a large scale. Things may also become less spontaneous, however, and the commercial world may start to dominate.

Sometimes we need to stop and ask whether this or that way of celebrating is appropriate. We enjoy giving and receiving gifts, but my friends celebrating their diamond wedding don't want gifts. Other than the gift of continuing their life together and good health, they have everything they need or desire, so they have asked for donations for the local hospice. On a larger scale, people are questioning whether or not burning effigies of those persecuted for their religious beliefs (as of Guy Fawkes on bonfire night) is acceptable when we need to promote respect and harmony between different faith communities.

All this now brings us to Christmas! The next two weeks of readings seek to help us delve more deeply into the meaning of celebrating Christmas and think about how, in a very commercialized context, we might celebrate Christ's birth appropriately.

David Spriggs

MARK 2:18–20 (CEV)

Why party anyway?

Some people came and asked Jesus, 'Why do the followers of John and those of the Pharisees often go without eating, while your disciples never do?' Jesus answered: 'The friends of a bridegroom don't go without eating while he is still with them. But the time will come when he will be taken from them. Then they will go without eating.'

When was the last time you went to a party? Don't be too narrow in your definition! While we still talk about christening and birthday 'parties', we tend to refer to wedding parties as 'banquets' or 'receptions'. Many call festivities to mark other achievements, whether retirement or the awarding of an OBE, a 'celebration'. All of these are different forms of parties, though. So what was yours?

Just as we have a whole range of reasons for partying, so does the Bible. One that is common to us all is a wedding. The way we celebrate a wedding, however, can vary from culture to culture. Some of us regard the tendency to spend £10,000 plus on a fairly ordinary wedding as extravagant, but for other cultures it is the norm.

Tony Campolo, a well-known American Christian speaker, owns up to his Italian roots when he writes: 'I have been to Jewish weddings. They are pretty much like Italian weddings. With all of us Mediterranean types, wedding receptions are the ultimate blow-out. I honestly believe that you don't know what partying is all about until you've been to one of our wedding receptions. Parents… will get into debt… to make sure that there is enough music, food and drink to keep everybody partying all night' (*The Kingdom of God Is a Party*, Paternoster, 1990).

Jesus was an honoured guest at a wedding party and used his God-given power to ensure that there was enough wine 'to keep everybody partying all night'—actually, for many days, for this was the Jewish custom at the time (John 2:1–11). Moreover, not only does Jesus relate the coming of the kingdom of God to a party, he implies that he can be considered the bridegroom. So, one reason to celebrate Christmas is that it heralds the beginning of the wedding!

Prayer

Lord, help us to make all our worship and celebrations this Christmas enjoyable for us and honouring to you.

DS

Why party? Achievements

Jesus told the people another story: 'What will a woman do if she has ten silver coins and loses one of them? Won't she light a lamp, sweep the floor, and look carefully until she finds it? Then she will call in her friends and neighbours and say, "Let's celebrate! I've found the coin I lost."' Jesus said, 'In the same way God's angels are happy when even one person turns to him.'

Recently, my daughter was awarded her degree. This marked three years' hard work, as well as the opportunity to learn many skills, from cooking to confronting landlords! Achieving her BSc was marked in two significant ways. First came the degree ceremony when she, along with hundreds of others, proceeded in line to the stage, shook the vice-chancellor's hand and heard a speech. The real celebration came later, though— the all-night ball with dressing up, socializing, photographs, eating, music and dancing. A party!

The Bible also recognizes that achievements should be marked with parties. Finding a sheep out on the Judean hillside was a significant achievement, requiring blood, sweat and tears. The anxiety (would the wolf get there first?) and uncertainty (would the sheep be visible if it had fallen down a ravine?) both deepened the joy of success, justifying a neighbourhood party (see Luke 15:1–7). Similarly, managing to find a small coin (part of the wedding dowry for this poor Jewish woman), after searching all the crevices of the floor and walls in a dark house, was an unexpected achievement. Calling friends and neighbours round for a party was a natural way to express her joy.

It was not only small-scale domestic incidents that warranted parties then. Grander achievements, such as military conquest, certainly did, too. It is in this light that we can consider how the birth of Jesus warrants a party, for his coming was the result of endless years of preparation and marked a most significant step on God's route to re-establishing his reign on earth. It is something to celebrate. That is what the angel is saying to the shepherds: 'Don't be afraid! I have good news for you' (Luke 2:10). 'Good news' was almost a technical term for 'victory' or 'achievement'.

Reflection

How important is it that we understand the reason for a celebration?

DS

LUKE 7:36, 44–46 (CEV, ABRIDGED)

Why party? Honoured guests

A Pharisee invited Jesus to have dinner with him. So Jesus went to the Pharisee's home and got ready to eat... He... said to Simon, '...When I came into your home, you didn't give me any water so I could wash my feet... You didn't greet me with a kiss... You didn't even pour olive oil on my head.'

When Abraham received three heavenly visitors, he wanted to acknowledge their status by providing them with a party (Genesis 18:1–8). It was the Eastern way of expressing—both in practical and social terms—the privilege he felt and the respect he wanted to give. When Simon the Pharisee invited Jesus to his home, this was the background custom that he was employing, even if his motives were rather less honourable, for he saw this close encounter as an opportunity to test Jesus' veracity.

When the prodigal son returned home, his father wanted to express not only his joy at his son's safe return from oblivion but also his public restoration of this wayward son by honouring him with a party (Luke 15:11–32). No wonder the older brother was furious as well as hurt. The faithful service and loyal obedience over many years of the son who had stayed at home was being spurned while his dissolute brother was publicly fêted in the most overt and extravagant manner. He was being restored to his son-ship and, the older brother feared, to a half of the remaining inheritance. That is why the father is quick to reassure him that his inheritance remains intact: 'My son, you are always with me, and everything I have is yours. But we should be glad and celebrate!' (vv. 31–32).

The angels announced to the shepherds that an honoured guest had just arrived in Bethlehem: 'This very day in King David's home town a Saviour was born for you. He is Christ the Lord' (Luke 2:11). The Christ or Messiah was not merely an honoured guest, he was *the* honoured guest—the one for whom Israel had been waiting for hundreds of years. He was the most prestigious guest imaginable because he was God's chosen agent to bring restoration to Israel. Partying is a very appropriate response to such amazing news!

Prayer

Lord, forgive us if sometimes in our Christmas celebrations we forget who we are honouring.

DS

DEUTERONOMY 14:22–23, 26–27 (CEV, ABRIDGED)

Why party? Religious celebrations

People of Israel, every year you must set aside ten per cent of your grain harvest… your wine and olive oil, and the firstborn of every cow, sheep, and goat. Take these to the place where the Lord chooses to be worshipped… When you and your family arrive, spend the money on food for a big celebration… remember to ask the Levites to celebrate with you.

Israel was accustomed to celebrating major festivals and events with parties. When we use words such as 'sacrifice' in association with such events in biblical times, we think mainly of the cost or death of the sacrificial lamb. While this was part of the picture, it was, perhaps, not the dominant feature for those who experienced these things. It was more like party time.

Those who presented their tithes were to eat them at the sanctuary to remind them that all they had came from God and, therefore, they should love him with all their heart, soul, mind and strength and respond to him with obedience to his commands. Part of the mechanism for stimulating their obedience was that they had such a good time in the sanctuary! If the people lived too far away to carry all their tithes and drive their animals such a long distance, they were allowed to sell the produce and take the money instead. However, they were not simply to give the money to the temple: 'When you and your family arrive, spend the money on food for a big celebration' (v. 26).

The importance of this 'partying' experience is reinforced by a passage in Nehemiah. The people have been so disturbed by listening to God's laws and recognizing their disobedience that they burst into deep, repentant wailing. Nehemiah and Ezra respond saying: 'This is a special day for the Lord your God. So don't be sad and don't cry!… Enjoy your good food and wine and share some with those who didn't have anything to bring' (Nehemiah 8:9–10).

As we have already seen, the angel told the shepherds that this was a special day for God—it would become a significant memory for God's people, shaping their response to him. It was a reason for joy then and is a reason for parties now.

Reflection

Does the way we celebrate Christmas reflect the joy of the Lord?

DS

Why party? Coronations

All at once an angel came down to them [the shepherds] from the Lord, and the brightness of the Lord's glory flashed around them. The shepherds were frightened. But the angel said, 'Don't be afraid! I have good news for you, which will make everyone happy. This very day in King David's home town a Saviour was born for you. He is Christ the Lord.'

I was only seven in 1953 (now there's a giveaway!). Nevertheless, I can still remember vividly the hysteria of celebration that affected our village and, from what I have gathered later, the whole nation, as Princess Elizabeth became Queen. People came together to plan elaborate street parties, while we massed in the village hall for our local celebration. Streets were festooned with flags and white bread sandwiches and substantial cakes were produced in vast numbers. I cannot remember what we had to drink, as it was so long ago that Coke had not reached us!

Coronations were important in the ancient world, too. If you showed any hesitation in your celebrations or failed to provide resources, it was liable to be read as, at best, a lack of support for the new monarch and, at worst, treason! So, partying was the order of the day for a new king, but also for the birth of the heir to his throne—as this ensured (in theory at least) the continuation of the dynasty and reduced the risk of hostile takeover bids!

When the angel announced to the shepherds that Christ the Lord had been born, the choir emphasized God's investment in this 'heir to the throne' with their chorus of, 'Praise God in heaven! Peace on earth to everyone who pleases God' (Luke 2:14). In this we can hear echoes of the earthly monarch's delight at the birth of a son, even the implicit warning in the final clause to any who thought otherwise. Here, then, is another reason to party at the birth of Jesus: the heir to the throne has arrived safely. God and all in heaven rejoice in this event. All on Earth are encouraged to respond joyfully, too.

Prayer

Lord, as we and the whole nation prepare to celebrate Christmas, help us to recognize more clearly that you are the Christ.

DS

MATTHEW 22:2–7 (CEV, ABRIDGED)

Why party? Beware!

The kingdom of heaven is like what happened when a king gave a wedding banquet for his son. The king sent some servants to tell the invited guests to come to the banquet, but the guests refused. He sent other servants to say to the guests, 'The banquet is ready! My cattle and prize calves have all been prepared...' But the guests did not pay any attention... Others grabbed the servants... and killed them... This made the king so furious that he sent an army to kill those murderers and burn down their city.

Have you ever received an invitation to a wedding, birthday or anniversary celebration and either couldn't go or didn't want to do so? It can be hard to find gracious words to decline the invitation so as not to offend the people who asked you. Whatever you say, it means that you are putting someone or something before them!

When it's the monarch inviting you to the crown prince's wedding, you are in much bigger trouble! There is, in fact, no proper or polite way to say 'No'. In the East you didn't even have the excuse that you couldn't get ready in time because you would have been given advance notice. An invitation would be issued some time before the actual event and then a summons once everything was ready, which is why the servants are sent to tell the guests that the banquet is ready.

Neither carrying on as though you have not heard, nor killing the messengers so that you can claim you haven't heard will work. It means that you are slighting the king at best, initiating a rebellion at worst. Hence, the severe punishment the king ordains for those who refuse his invitation.

The response of the shepherds to the angels (Luke 2:15) is a model one. Although they were legally responsible for the sheep's care, they instantly decide to journey to find out what is going on—to join the party, so to speak. We should be careful that all the business that Christmas generates—shopping, presents and parties—means that we have no time or energy to respond eagerly to God's invitation to us through Christmas.

Prayer

O God, help us to hear your voice through all the noise of Christmas and, having heard, make you our priority.

DS

Exodus 32:3–6 (CEV, abridged)

Why party? Behave!

Everybody took off their earrings... [Aaron] melted them and made an idol in the shape of a young bull... he built an altar in front of the idol and said, 'Tomorrow we will celebrate in honour of the Lord.' The people got up early the next morning and killed some animals to be used for sacrifices and others to be eaten. Then everyone ate and drank so much that they began to carry on like wild people.

We have seen that, in the light of who Jesus is, there are many reasons for partying to celebrate his birth. He is the newborn king, an honoured guest; his birth initiates a new religious phase and so on. Nevertheless, we should not overlook the fact that the way in which we party matters, as Aaron found out.

Aaron and the people thought that they were honouring God. They regarded the idol, which they had constructed at considerable personal sacrifice, as 'the god [don't forget that in Hebrew there are no upper-case letters—it is only in English that we distinguish between 'God' and 'god'] who brought us out of Egypt!' (v. 4). The intention was to 'celebrate in honour of the Lord' (v. 5). Although they did celebrate with sacrifices, it all went wrong: 'everyone ate and drank so much that they began to carry on like wild people' (v. 6)— wild people whom God denigrates as 'acting like fools' (v. 7).

Can we pinpoint the problems? First, tired of waiting, the people had constructed a God to their own design—they wanted a god who was readily available and who would please them. We need to be alert in case the Christ we bring to Christmas is one of our own imagining and not the true Christ, who must suffer and then enter his glory (Luke 24:26). Second, their behaviour was not only exuberant but also excessive—they had lost control of themselves and probably serious sexual immorality was involved. If our Christmas partying becomes an excuse for overindulgence, selfish hedonism and immorality, it is offensive to God and dishonours Christ.

Reflection

How can we truly celebrate this most joyful event both in and for human life and, at the same time, do so in a way that truly respects and reflects the nature of God?

DS

Deuteronomy 14:28–29; Nehemiah 8:10 (CEV, abridged)

Good party? The guests

Every third year, instead of using the ten per cent of your harvest for a big celebration… put it into a community storehouse. The Levites have no land of their own, so you must give them food… also give food to the poor who live in your town, including orphans, widows, and foreigners. If they have enough to eat, then the Lord your God will be pleased.

Nehemiah told the people, 'Enjoy your good food and wine and share some with those who don't have anything to bring… This is a special day for the Lord.'

One of the most important features of a party is the people—if no one's there, it's not going to be much of a party! Equally, if the people are boring or badly behaved, we're not likely to want to go. Imagine that you have been invited to a party where your favourite radio or TV presenter, or even footballer or film star, will be and that you will spend the evening with them. That might be quite an enticement.

One of the joys of Christmas can be the chance to be with brothers and sisters, aunts and uncles, grandparents, cousins and others we have not seen for months, catching up on their news and enjoying each other's company.

For some of us, one of the values of parties is that we can meet someone new. Parties provide opportunities for discovery—we might even meet our future spouse.

As well as the Old Testament passages above, Jesus taught that when we give parties, we should invite those who are unlikely to ever repay the compliment—the sick, social outcasts, beggars and so forth (see Luke 14:16–24, for example). Some churches are very good at providing Christmas meals and other festivities for either lonely people or those who are homeless. Many, too, are involved in distributing Christmas presents and food to those who are less well off—another way of taking the party to the people.

As Christians, keeping a focus on the people at the party is a core way to celebrate, not least because Christ's promise to us is that in others we may find him (Matthew 25:37–40).

Sunday prayer

Help us, Lord, to see you and serve you in other people who are excluded for whatever reason from Christmas celebrations.

DS

Good party? The guests' clothes

When the king went in to meet the guests, he found that one of them was not wearing the right kind of clothes for the wedding. The king asked, 'Friend, why didn't you wear proper clothes for the wedding?' But the guest had no excuse. So the king gave orders for that person to be tied hand and foot and to be thrown outside into the dark.

Ours is a very informal age. Open-necked shirts with suits are the uniform for TV presenters and even at a prestigious advertising agency in London the receptionists may well wear jeans and T-shirts, as my daughter discovered when she turned up for an interview—in her new suit.

Yet, even today, there are exceptions to this informality. If you are invited to Buckingham Palace, you wear what is prescribed; for a family wedding a fortune may well be spent not only on the clothes and hats, but on all the other personal preparations—hair, manicures, even fake suntans! We don't only spend money, we also spend time. To fail to be properly dressed for these occasions is an implicit insult to our hosts.

This understanding lies behind the host in the passage's angry reaction when he discovers someone who hasn't bothered to get properly dressed for the wedding banquet. It was an insult to both kingdom and occasion.

When the shepherds arrived at the stable, they would still have been in their dirty working clothes, but that didn't matter, for when it comes to Christ's party it is a different kind of dress that takes priority. Gentleness, kindness, humility, meekness, patience, tolerance, forgiveness and, especially, love are the dress code for God's kingdom (see Colossians 3:12–14, NRSV—the image here is of putting on clothes). The shepherds also brought an excitement and keen desire to discover more of this mystery. People who go to parties that celebrate the birth of God's son 'dressed' like this will be more than welcome.

Whether the party we have in view is the office party or a service of nine lessons and carols, we do well to spend as long preparing our inner Christian dress as we would our outward appearance for a wedding.

Prayer

Lord, may the words we speak, the attention we show and the values we display, be worthy of the King whose birth we celebrate.

DS

Luke 15:22; 2:11–12 (CEV)

Good party? The chief guest's clothes

But his father said to the servants, 'Hurry and bring the best clothes and put them on him. Give him a ring for his finger and sandals for his feet.' … [The angel said] 'This very day in King David's home town a Saviour was born for you. He is Christ the Lord. You will know who he is, because you will find him dressed in baby's clothes and lying on a bed of hay.'

Whether it's the Oscars or a royal occasion, the main focus for the TV cameras and the press commenting on them is to answer the question 'What are they wearing?' Is it too flamboyant or understated or revealing?

The father in Jesus' parable wanted his younger son to know, together with everyone in the household, that he was treating him as an honoured guest, not an errant member of the family. The best clothes signal the honour that the father is bestowing on him.

In the kingdom of God, the Son is dressed in ordinary peasant clothes. Herod would not have allowed his own son and heir to be dressed in strips of cloth and Herod would have made sure that the place where his child slept looked more like a throne than a cradle, let alone a 'bed of hay'.

God, though, was making sure, right from the start, that Jesus was to be thought of as one of us, claiming no special status, in human terms, nor being treated differently by God, insulated from normal realities, such as tiredness, work or the vulnerabilities of political upheaval and personal suffering.

It is right that our Christmas celebrations are full and richly enjoyable because it is the coming of the king that we celebrate, but, equally, we should seek to communicate the qualities of Jesus' own particular brand of kingship. Maybe guests at our Christmas services could be invited to give to a local charity for the underprivileged or one of the international aid agencies. Perhaps at our family Christmas meals we can include prayers or time of silence for those in our world in desperate need. Alternatively, we could display a large lit candle together with a poster from a charity and invite contributions.

Prayer

Lord Jesus Christ, only son of the Father, help us to honour you with consideration for the marginalized and generosity for the dispossessed.

DS

Good party? The welcome

The Word was in the world, but no one knew him, though God had made the world with his Word. He came into his own world, but his own nation did not welcome him. Yet some people accepted him and put their faith in him. So he gave them the right to be the children of God.

It can be so embarrassing if you arrive at a party or celebration and you sense either that you are far too early or, even worse, you were not expected at all. How we are welcomed can set the tone for the whole event for us. It can be draining trying to pretend that you are not there for several hours!

As we have seen, Jesus was invited to a party that was supposed to be in his honour, but as soon as he arrived he realized that it was more to do with the prestige of his host or his desire to interrogate Jesus. His host forgot to welcome him with the normal courtesies of foot washing and perfumed oils for the chief guest (Luke 7:36–50).

The Christmas story recognizes the importance of welcomes, too. John tells us that Jesus came to the world his father had made, but even his own people did not receive or welcome him (1:11.) Mary and Joseph struggled to find accommodation in David's city, which should surely have welcomed its new king. When the shepherds found Jesus, however, even though they were unexpected, they were welcomed, for when they blurted out their amazing story of angels 'everyone listened' and responded to them appropriately (Luke 2:18).

Welcoming our guests properly is part of true Christmas celebrations. Most churches now do greet people with a smile and cheery word, but can we make the welcome more fulsome for those who don't normally attend our churches? Should we, for instance, start (instead of finish) the proceedings informally with drinks and mince pies before we settle down for worship? Research indicates that 'non-church' people would often consider this more normal than the traditional format.

Reflection

'Whenever you did it for any of my people, no matter how unimportant they seemed, you did it for me' (Matthew 25:40). How can we convey to our unexpected guests that they are really welcome, to us as well as Jesus?

DS

LUKE 15:25–27 (CEV)

Good party? The festivities

The elder son had been out in the field. But when he came near the house, he heard the music and dancing. So he called one of the servants over and asked, 'What's going on here?' The servant answered, 'Your brother has come home safe and sound, and your father ordered us to kill the best calf.'

We live not far from our village hall. On a summer's evening we can tell when there is a good party going on because not only the music but also the sound of human laughter, excited voices and general enjoyment drift towards us. Similar sounds reached the weary farmer as he made his way home after an intense day's toil under the hot sun. He was perplexed when he heard the noise, because it was not harvest time so what possible reason could there be for such celebration?

Just as the household celebrated the lost son's return, so it is appropriate that, as we celebrate the coming of God's son among us, we should have a rich diet of festivities. For some people this is epitomized in a dignified carol service with plenty of traditional music, for others it is summed up by young schoolchildren's attempts at 'Away in a manger' or a nativity play. Surely, though, there is room for much more varied ways of celebrating. Why not a Christmas jazz concert with wine?

Why not rap our way through the Christmas story? Why not enjoy food and music from around the world? Why not dress the church in the flags of all the nations? Why not let your imagination run wild as you dream of new and exciting ways to celebrate the birth of the king of kings and lord of lords, not only in church but everywhere? As long as the quality and the tone communicate that this is an exceptional moment in our human story, then surely every expression of communal joy counts.

What matters even more is that if someone asks us, 'What's going on here?', like the servant in the story, we have an answer, for our hope—Jesus, God's Son, the saviour of the world—has been born for us!

Prayer

Glorious God, may all our Christmas celebrations overflow with your joy, love and vitality, so that many people will stop and ask, 'What's going on here?'

DS

2 Corinthians 9:11–15 (CEV, abridged)

Good party? The presents

You will be blessed in every way, and you will be able to keep on being generous. Then many people will thank God when we deliver your gift... The way in which you have proved yourselves by this service will bring honour and praise to God. You believed the message about Christ, and you obeyed it by sharing generously with God's people and with everyone else... Thank God for his gift that is too wonderful for words!

Presents dominate the landscape of Christmas. No doubt the three gifts of the Magi would be cited if we asked people why this is so, even though Jesus had to wait a year or two to get them. As for the shepherds, in spite of the assumption of many nativity plays, there is no hint that they brought lambs.

Yet, giving is still at the heart of Christmas. The supreme giver gave the perfect present, communicating love at infinite cost. God's gift 'that is too wonderful for words' is the real stimulus for giving.

Many factors contribute to the appreciation of any gift. It may depend on the giver and how much they matter to us—think of children's or grandchildren's handmade gifts. Sometimes it's the usefulness or because it 'spoils us', thus affirming our worth. Sometimes it's the 'wow' factor, when the present is something we really wanted, showing that the giver understood us. Somewhere in the mix is also the cost—not primarily in the monetary sense, but in the time, ingenuity and love expended. The best gifts indicate that the giver has in some way given of themselves to us.

We can reflect a little of God's generosity by providing presents for children and adults who have little via 'toy services', giving to charities that express God's love in practical ways and spending time with people who feel neglected.

Can we help our children discover the heart of Christmas giving by providing a present for them to give away to someone else, perhaps at a church service or Christmas party? Can we discover the heart of Christmas by giving the gift of telling someone about the love of God or inviting them to come and see the one who is their saviour, too?

Prayer

Lord Jesus Christ, son of the Father, as you have blessed us, so help us bless others at this Christmas season.

DS

Good party? Looking forward

'This very day in King David's home town a Saviour was born for you.' … Then he [Simeon] blessed them and told Mary, 'This child of yours will cause many people in Israel to fall and others to stand.' … The child Jesus grew. He became strong and wise, and God blessed him.

Whether it's a new motorway opened or a new boat commissioned, there will be a celebration. It is natural for us to want to celebrate new beginnings. We have already seen that there are many aspects to celebrating the new beginning that Christmas commemorates. There is one danger to avoid as well, however.

If the shepherds had returned from their angelic encounter and its exciting confirmation in the stable and thought, 'Well, that's it, then', it would have been desperately sad. The angel did not say, 'There's a saviour for the day', but that their saviour had been born. The opening of a new motorway or the launch of a boat is indeed a cause for celebration, but mainly because it opens up new possibilities for the future, for quicker travel or enjoyable cruises.

As we finish our Christmas holidays and enter the new year, we take our celebrations with us. Jesus is still the same saviour—yesterday, today and always. It was wonderful that the shepherds received clear confirmation of the angel's message when they found the baby, but they returned home praising God for his promises for the future as well as the recent memories of the new arrival (Luke 2:20). They knew that they were special, and that God was at work in their times; they could look forward with hope because their daily journey would then be in the company of their saviour.

They did not know what would happen. In some ways, the days would probably have appeared much the same as before, but life as a whole would be different. God had given them their special encounter with Jesus to bring sparkle to the ordinary, strength for their challenges and hope when everything seemed dark. We have the same saviour.

Prayer

Lord God, as we journey through this year, may the joy of Christmas celebrations come to mind when life is dull or difficult and rekindle in us the certainty that we have a wonderful saviour. Amen

DS

New Daylight

Magazine

Sound the trumpet!

Stephen Rand

'On the Day of Atonement [or Great Day of Forgiveness, CEV] sound the trumpet throughout your land. Consecrate the fiftieth year and proclaim liberty throughout the land to all its inhabitants. It shall be a jubilee for you' (Leviticus 25:9–10).

The experts say that our word 'Jubilee' comes from the Hebrew word for the sound made by the ram's horn trumpet. And that's the sound that announces God's intervention in human history. It was the sound heard by the citizens of Jericho before the walls of their city collapsed; it is the sound that will announce the second coming of Christ.

The year of Jubilee was enshrined in God's law as a time of intervention on behalf of the poor. Every fifty years, the trumpet would sound and herald new hope for those who were in debt and destitute. Imagine that you were one of those struggling against the odds, every meal eked out of backbreaking labour on unresponsive soil—but knowing that there was a promise of a new start. Your ears would have strained for the sound, the moment when things would change. When Jesus began his ministry, he referred to this same moment, quoting Isaiah 61: 'The Spirit of the Lord is on me, because he has anointed me to preach good news to the poor' (Luke 4:18).

This is why Jubilee became the inspiration for a movement that longed for a new start for the world's poor: to celebrate the start of a new millennium by setting them free from the chains of debt. *Jubilee 2000* set out to change the world; its story is a testament to the power of biblical inspiration to motivate ordinary people to make a difference.

Politicians and economists thought that world debt was too complicated for people to get excited about, but towards the end of the 1990s it was summed up in one simple fact: that for every pound that was given in aid to the developing world, three pounds were coming back to pay off debt. This was sufficient to create a burning sense of injustice, a determination that something must be done. People were scandalized that there were countries spending more on debt payments to the rich than on the health and education of their own people.

The problem stemmed from oil. The price rises of the 1970s left the banks full of cash that they wanted to lend, and what could be better than loans to poor countries to help them become wealthy? Then interest rates spiralled and commodity prices fell, and many countries were left effectively bankrupt, owing far more than they could earn. In some cases this was exacerbated by corrupt dictators, whose families were enriched beyond their wildest dreams. Even when their citizens ejected them from office, those citizens were left to pay off the debts from which they had seen little or no benefit.

The problem stemmed from oil

This was no abstract mathematical problem. It meant that as countries became desperate to raise the money to pay their debts, charges were introduced for health care and education. Mothers suddenly had to choose between feeding their family or sending their children to school. Life-saving medicine was available only if you could afford it. The debt crisis was a crisis of poverty—poverty that means 30,000 people die every day, unnecessarily.

What could be done? How could the leaders of the world's richest nations be convinced that action was a moral imperative in the face of such injustice and suffering? It was an enormous challenge. The 1990s were years when the richest nations got richer, and their willingness to help the poorest lessened.

But a small group of Christians took up the challenge. They knew that it needed the support of people both inside and outside the churches. They knew that it needed a global movement to bring global change. They knew that it needed a unique coalition of religious organizations, aid agencies, trade unions and campaigning groups to get the message out. Consciously seeing debt as a modern form of slavery, they picked up a strategy that had been key to the anti-slavery campaign 200 years earlier: a petition. The Jubilee petition called on the G8, the leaders of the world's richest nations, to cancel the unpayable debt of the world's poorest nations under a fair and transparent process.

I can still remember carrying box after box of petitions from a boat to the location of the G8 leaders' meeting in Cologne, Germany, in 1999. I was one of a chain gang, linked by shackles on our ankles, symbolizing the message of the petition that the chains of debt would be broken. It had been signed by 24.3 million people from over 160 countries—the world's first global campaign. 233,000 signed the petition on European Election day in Britain.

The petition reinforced the impact of the human chain created by 70,000 campaigners that welcomed the G8 leaders to Birmingham in 1998. It was peaceful, cheerful, determined and unprecedented—and it made a difference.

The world has been changed. Poverty is on the world's agenda as it never has been before. There is an expectation that world leaders will act on behalf of people in need. In 2000, at a special session of the United Nations, the world's countries adopted the Millennium Development Goals, promising action to halve world poverty by 2015.

And there was specific action on debt: an enhanced debt relief initiative intended to set countries free of the burden of debt. Last year I read a letter from the President of Tanzania to the annual conference of *Jubilee Debt Campaign*. He wrote to express his thanks for the campaign, and the difference it had made in his country:

When I became President in 1995, we were witnessing a serious deterioration of social services, and a high and unsustainable debt burden. One of my first priorities was to reverse these trends through increasing government revenue and asking for debt relief… Now the primary school population has increased by 66 per cent; we have built 45,000 classrooms and 1925 new primary schools; we have recruited 37,261 new teachers between 2000 and 2004, and retrained another 14,852.

'Together we have achieved much, but much remains to be done'

What an encouragement to know that there are such tangible results to the campaign! In 27 countries, billions of dollars have been redirected to make a real impact on the lives of poor people. In many countries, new ways have been established of involving ordinary people in ensuring that money is spent where it makes the most impact. Research shows that it really has been spent on the priorities of poverty, not on the army, and not corruptly lost to bureaucrats and politicians.

So why is *Jubilee Debt Campaign* still campaigning? President Mkapa's letter went on, 'Together we have achieved much; but much remains to be done.' Children are still dying unnecessarily because of poverty. Poor countries are still being sued by commercial companies for the repayment of debt. There are heavily indebted countries still outside all debt relief programmes. There are lives being ruined by the economic policy conditions being demanded as the price of debt relief. The debt relief plans of 1999/2000 have failed to bring the new start for the poor that was needed. The trumpet sounded—but not nearly loud enough or long enough.

The need for action is still great. In September 2005, the United Nations meets to discuss progress on meeting the Millennium Development Goals. The prospects are grim. At the beginning of the year, Gordon Brown, the Chancellor of the Exchequer who has made this issue such a personal crusade, emphasized the remaining challenge:

And at best on present progress in Sub Saharan Africa: primary education for all will be delivered not in 2015 but 2130—that is 115 years too late; the halving of poverty not by 2015 but by 2150—that is 135 years too late; and the elimination of avoidable infant deaths not by 2015 but by 2165—that is 150 years too late. So when people ask how long, the whole world must reply: 150 years is too long to wait for justice; 150 years is too long to wait when infants are dying in Africa while the rest of the world has the medicines to heal them; 150 years is too long for people to wait when a promise should be redeemed, when the bond of trust should be honoured now in this decade.

2005 is a year of enormous challenge—and opportunity. A new coalition of faith groups, aid agencies, trade unions and others has been active through the year that has seen the UK once again act as hosts to the G8. *Jubilee Debt Campaign* has been a major player in this campaign to 'Make Poverty History'. We know that if we are to seize this historic moment for good, then there has to be the political will for the richest nations in the world to stand for justice and act with generosity. Debt has to be cancelled. There needs to be more and better aid. And there needs to be a new recognition of the need for trade justice, that will see the poorest nations given the opportunity to use their resources for the benefit of their own people.

Promises have been made. They need to be kept. The *Jubilee Debt Campaign* has shown that when people raise their voice against injustice, change is possible. But it is not inevitable. The calling of all Christians is to make the commitment to the long haul, inspired by the vision of what could be and should be. We pray, 'Your kingdom come, your will be done.' It's such a great discovery when we realize that God wants to empower us to fulfil his will and become part of the answer to our own prayers.

Stephen Rand is Co-Chair of Jubilee Debt Campaign. For more information go to:
www.jubileedebtcampaign.org.uk
or ring 020 7324 4722.

Barnabas: ten years old this year!

Lucy Moore

Ten years ago I was knee-deep in nappies and wondering what God had in mind for my life. Ten years ago BRF was launching its very first *Barnabas* book and wondering where God would take it from there.

Ten years on, both BRF and I are on the brink of coping with adolescents: me as I send the twelve-year-old off to brave secondary school, and BRF as the *Barnabas* Team throws itself into the equivalent of staying out late and bringing home friends to devour the contents of the pantry.

Yes, staying out late, and—though not known as a teenage fault—getting up horribly early. So you might ask why on earth the members of the *Barnabas* Team do a job in which they find themselves on the M4 in the fog even before *Farming Today* has come on air!

Perhaps one of the answers is that what *Barnabas* offers is unique, and it's exhilarating to be part of a pioneering and dynamic organization that's really scratching where it itches. We're able to work on a professional level with schools and churches as we bring the Bible to life through the creative arts.

The early starts and late nights might be gruelling but it's a fact that *Barnabas* is becoming known and respected across the UK, and worth the travel in order to reach all corners. Recently, at the national RE Advisers' Conference, there was a real groundswell of approval among these influential people from all over England and Wales for what *Barnabas* offers, and many unsolicited testimonies from advisers whose schools had enjoyed *Barnabas Live* days. I felt very proud to be part of an organization with this sort of reputation. With the injection of energy and talent from the Northern Team, we really do feel we're reaching the whole country.

And the work itself is rewarding. There aren't many jobs where you get to play in the 'Bible playground'. A workshop with five-year-olds in Gloucestershire on Christmas gave me plenty of opportunity to refresh my vision of the old story as they threw themselves instantly and wholeheartedly into the story. It's also a privilege to be at hand when children are thinking through answers to huge questions: 'Perhaps Abraham couldn't have had the baby if he didn't have to do all that waiting first.' Or to see the 'So impress me' eleven-year-olds at the back of the assembly hall actually look forward to their drama workshop, knowing that it's focused on the Bible.

I mentioned teenagers raiding the pantry: the *Barnabas* pantry is continually restocked with resources to satisfy the hungriest teacher or children's worker. It's great to have this supply of high-quality books to offer to adults alongside the face-to-face ministry—and to see people become confident and enthusiastic about opening up the Bible in all the stimulating ways they come across through *Barnabas*. We always enjoy the Road to Damascus moments, when teachers or leaders see our ideas slotting into place within their work: 'Oooh! I could use that in my all-age worship!' 'That Quiet Day changed my life…'

It's wonderful to see people of all ages relax into a story from the Bible and to trust that it will take root in their lives. Whether it's the laughter of a bouncy version of David and Goliath, with teachers being slain by a child from Year 2, or the charged stillness around a *Godly Play* story of creation, being in a position to bring the stories of the Bible to life is a privilege, both as a performer and as a Christian.

You may wonder how you can be part of this work yourself. Well, there are three ways. We would love you to pray for us: it's lonely out on the road and in new situations, and knowing that people are praying for us is a big encouragement. Why not register with the BRF office to get our bi-monthly Prayer Letter?

You could also help us to make the work more widely known by passing information on to others who may be interested—perhaps your school or church cluster. It really does make a difference for a school to receive a leaflet from someone they know and trust, rather than getting it cold through the post.

And lastly, we are working with some of the most under-funded groups in the country and do our best to keep our charges as low as possible, so we rely on donations. Your financial support can enable 21st-century children to get excited about the Bible and to allow God's word to change attitudes, behaviour, even society in the long term.

Ten years old, growing all the time in the range and scope of what we can offer and how far we can travel, with books reaching as far as Paraguay and Australia and ministry from Truro to Sunderland, *Barnabas* is looking forward to what God will do with us in the next ten years.

BRF's Barnabas work is funded mainly through donations and grants from churches and individual supporters. To make a donation, see the form on page 156.

An extract from
O Come, Emmanuel

Gordon Giles

BRF's Advent book for 2005 is by Gordon Giles, who has also written *The Harmony of Heaven* (2003) and *The Music of Praise* (2002). *O Come, Emmanuel* presents daily reflections on a wide range of music associated with the Advent and Christmas season, as well as relevant Bible readings. Here is the (slightly abridged) reading for 6 December, which features a well-known hymn.

Benjamin Britten: St Nicholas

'The saying is sure: whoever aspires to the office of bishop desires a noble task. Now a bishop must be above reproach, married only once, temperate, sensible, respectable, hospitable, an apt teacher, not a drunkard, not violent but gentle, not quarrelsome, and not a lover of money. He must manage his own household well, keeping his children submissive and respectful in every way—for if someone does not know how to manage his own household, how can he take care of God's church? He must not be a recent convert, or he may be puffed up with conceit and fall into the condemnation of the devil. Moreover, he must be well thought of by outsiders, so that he may not fall into disgrace and the snare of the devil' *(1 Timothy 3:1–7)*.

God moves in a mysterious way
His wonders to perform;
He plants his footsteps in the sea,
And rides upon the storm…

Ye fearful saints, fresh courage take,
The clouds ye so much dread
Are big with mercy, and shall break
In blessings on your head.

Judge not the Lord by feeble sense,
But trust him for his grace;
Behind a frowning providence
He hides a smiling face.

His purposes will ripen fast,
Unfolding every hour;
The bud may have a bitter taste,
But sweet will be the flower…

Words: William Cowper (1731–1800)
Tune: 'London New' melody from the *Scottish Psalter* (1635), adapted in Playford's *Psalmes* (1671)

In many European countries, the feast of St Nicholas (Santa Claus) is celebrated on 6 December. Unlike the Swiss and Austrians (for example), the British do not generally make much of St Nicholas' day, preferring to note in passing that he was Bishop of Myra in the early fourth century (Nicholas is said to have been born in Patara, in AD260). Myra is very close to the modern Turkish city of Demre, and he was buried in the basilica there. In 1087 it was attacked and plundered by Italian sailors who took his remains to Bari in southern Italy, where his shrine still stands in the Cathedral of St Nicholas.

By the sixth century, Nicholas had aroused a certain following, and in the ninth century Methodius of Constantinople articulated some of the legends that had sprung up about his life and works. The cult of Nicholas grew, and by the 13th century, when Jacobus de Voragine (1228–98) collected together his *Legende Sanctorum* (*Legends of the Saints*) between 1255 and 1266, Nicholas' reputation was firmly established. Nicholas' popularity was strong in England in the eleventh and twelfth centuries, largely because of the influence of the Archbishop of Canterbury, St Anselm, and the long-lived hermit St Godric, both of whom wrote poetry or prayers in his honour. Godric's poem is one of the earliest examples of lyric poetry in English, and he is also reputed to have composed a musical accompa-

niment, which would make him the author of the first known music for English words... St Anselm, who was Archbishop of Canterbury from 1093 until his death in 1109, actually visited the city of Bari in Italy around the time that Nicholas' remains were stolen from Turkey and taken there. Back in England, he too championed St Nicholas' reputation.

The *Legende Sanctorum* was translated in 1450 and became one of the first books printed in English by William Caxton, under the title *The Golden Legend*. Interest in the book was revived when William Morris reprinted it in 1892. By then, St Nicholas' name had evolved into Santa Claus in American use, via the Dutch version of his name, *Sint Klaus*, and he became a figure of great interest. Connecting all the legends together was a recurring theme—of St Nicholas' special patronage of sailors, and of children.

Thus St Nicholas was an ideal choice as the subject of a cantata intended to be sung by a children's choir. The composer was Benjamin Britten (1913–76), whose friend, the tenor Peter Pears, had been a pupil at Lancing College in West Sussex. The College was celebrating its centenary in 1948, and Britten was commissioned to produce the work... Britten enjoyed composing the 50-minute work so much that it was basically complete in three weeks. What delighted him was the fact that he was writing music for amateurs and children to perform. This presented particular difficulties, but it also inspired him to produce a completely new type of musical work.

The part of Nicholas is taken by a tenor soloist, who gives us an insight into the ministry of an episcopal saint. He laments the condition of humanity and the prevalence of sin, but also accepts his own death with hope and courage. In the Introduction, we meet Nicholas, as though across time, who encourages us to preserve and teach the faith that still lives in us. The choir sing a prayer asking God for strength to serve.

Then we travel back 1600 years to 'The birth of Nicholas', where, apparently, his love of water, whether in bath or font, is manifest. Punctuating the movement is Nicholas' youthful cry, 'God be glorified', and at the end it is the tenor soloist, representing the adult saint, who takes up the call. This leads into a movement en-titled 'Nicholas devotes himself to God'. Here he reflects on the poverty of humanity, destined to die in fear of everlasting death. Nicholas sells his land to feed the hungry, but still has an 'angry soul'. Discordant music here gives way to musical resolution, telling us that God has heard his prayer.

The fourth section, 'He journeys to Palestine', recounts a sea voyage. Nicholas predicts a storm, but is mocked by the crew. That night a storm does arise, and the sailors are stricken and eventually turn to prayer. Nicholas joins them in praying for the storm to cease, and soon the waves are quelled and peace is restored. The movement ends as Nicholas thanks God for their deliverance.

The fifth movement sees Nicholas arrive in Myra, where he is chosen as bishop. Mitre, robes, crozier and episcopal ring are given to him amid great celebration. Then, in an unusual twist of convention, the audience stand to join in the well-known hymn based on Psalm 100: 'All people that on earth do dwell'. This involvement of the audience turns them into a dramatic congregation—the flock for whom Nicholas is chief pastor.

In the sixth movement, 'Nicholas from prison', we meet Nicholas as victim of Roman persecution. He has to celebrate communion with prison bread, but his fervour is still strong. He admonishes those who continue in sin, entreating them to bow down before God. Then, in the seventh movement, we move away from the prison as the choir tell of some travellers wandering without food. Three women call for Timothy, Mark and John, their missing sons. At an inn, the travellers order a meal, but Nicholas realizes that the meat they are to be served is actually the flesh of the three boys, who have been killed and pickled in salt. Nicholas calls them back to life and they enter, praising God and singing Alleluias.

Nicholas' good deeds are the subject of the eighth movement, 'His piety and marvellous works'. Now he is an old man, having been bishop for 40 years, and the choir sings of his devotion, courage and kindness. They remind us that he has saved them from imprisonment, hunger, shame, oppression and shipwreck. These deeds, the choir sings, should be kept alive in legend. Nicholas is soon to die, and in the final movement, 'The death of Nicholas', he hears his call and looks forward to the eternal life of heaven in union with Christ. The Nunc Dimittis is sung (Luke 2:29–32), and as the sound swells, the organ gently introduces a final hymn, 'God moves in a mysterious way'. Thus the cantata closes with this reminder of how we can never fully understand the workings of God, yet we can trust in his mercy and rely on him to bring us through the storms of life.

Whether we celebrate the feast of St Nicholas or not, there can be no doubt that he existed, even if some of the legends about him are quite elaborate. In one sense, we must say that Father Christmas exists!

The difficulty today comes when Santa Claus (Father Christmas) is confused with Jesus, such that many agonize over whether to tell their children about Santa Claus bringing presents. Children write to him, and a whole industry has arisen around the plastic patron saint of present-giving. If Santa Claus and Jesus are too closely associated, then there really is the risk that when children realize that Santa Claus is a modern commodity, they will throw the baby Jesus out with the bathwater-loving saint. A recent advertising campaign even portrayed Santa Claus in the manger, as a way of emphasizing the confusion that currently exists. 'Go on, ask him for something' read the caption. But in that image lies the fundamental truth and purpose about St Nicholas. For he, as a saint, would never have wanted attention on himself, but would have always desired to witness to Christ, his Lord and Saviour. Santa Claus witnesses to Christ, and we must never forget that.

So whatever we do, we should always tell children the truth about Santa Claus and, more importantly, the truth about Christ in the manger—Christ the baby, born to become the man who was to die for our salvation. This is the true belief of Christmas, shared by you and me, and by Santa Claus himself.

Prayer

O God, the Father of Christmas and of all time, send us your Holy Spirit, that we may be brought the gifts of love, joy and peace that you want for your children in this and every age, for the sake of your Son, Jesus Christ our Lord. Amen.

To order a copy of this book, please turn to the order form on page 159.

Recommended reading

Women of the Word

Looking at Bible passages from the perspective of the characters involved is an excellent way of bringing the text alive, especially in parts of the Old Testament where the stories may be challenging, not to say difficult, for today's sensibilities. As we read the Bible in this way, though, it can be all too easy to overlook many of the women characters.

While names such as Mary and Esther are familiar, what of Gomer and Abigail, Hagar and Sapphira, and those who are not named at all, despite the part they play? How much do we know about Lydia and Rhoda? About the Gentile woman who confronted Jesus, and the poor widow making her offering in the temple?

Women of the Word has its origin in one woman's decision to read through the Bible, cover to cover. Jackie Stead, editor of *Woman Alive* magazine, decided that she would read a few chapters one day, maybe no more than a few verses the next, carrying on each time until an insight leaped out from the page, which she would then note down for further reflection.

As she tells in the book's introduction, what happened was that almost from the beginning and the story of Eve, the insight that kept emerging was the extent to which

women get a 'raw deal', as she puts it. She continues:

Suddenly I was indignant that Sarai should have to pretend that she was Abram's sister rather than his wife, appalled that Lot would sacrifice his daughters to the baying crowd, and angry at the misery in the lives of both Leah and Rachel because of their father's trickery. The final straw was the story of Judah and Tamar in Genesis 38.

In summary, Tamar is a widow, who tricks her father-in-law Judah into sleeping with her, as he is failing in his duty to give her in marriage to his youngest son. She later gives birth to twin boys. Mulling over the story, Jackie goes on:

I wondered what I was supposed to take from it… It simply seemed to typify the harsh life and injustice that faced many of the women in the Bible. I began to think about other women's stories in the Bible. Surely I was missing something. I felt I wanted to understand them better.

As a result of her reflections, she decided in consultation with colleagues at the magazine to develop a series of Bible studies entitled 'Good Foundations', using a team of experienced writers to unpack some of the episodes featuring women and seeing how they can speak to people today. Fifteen of those original studies have been brought together in *Women of the Word*.

As well as considering lesser-known characters, the book picks up the perspectives of some of those who are not even named. BRF's own Kristina Petersen, one of the contributors to the original 'Good Foundations' series, writes on the Israelite slave girl who plays a key role in the story of the army commander Naaman in 2 Kings 5, suggesting that he visit the Israelite prophet Elisha to seek healing from his skin disease.

Kristina draws parallels with the fact that we too can make a difference, no matter how insignificant we may feel:

Do you ever feel that you have no influence, maybe not even many choices? … God's economy is different and those who are insignificant in the world's eyes can be used as powerfully by God as any king or ruler, any politician or leader or boardroom member. All the girl did was to hold on

to her faith and her integrity in adverse circumstances. She cared for those around her because she realized that they too were fragile human beings in need of God.

There is a moving reflection by Anne Roberts on the Gospel story of the women with the issue of blood, describing how her condition made her a social outcast, yet Jesus reached out in response to her faith and healed her when all she did was to touch the hem of his robe. Anne suggests that we can 'bring the hem of Jesus' garment' to somebody who feels outcast in our society, encouraging them to reach out and experience Christ's healing. She concludes, 'There is no kinder ministry… to those who are hurting through abuse and misunderstanding. Those who have done it for us have done what lightly made promises of prayer and protestations of love without action could never do. They bring us Jesus.'

Women of the Word is a highly accessible introduction to viewing the Bible from the perspective of some of these female characters, who have spent too long on the sidelines of church teaching. It is particularly suitable for readers who may never have ventured beyond daily Bible reading notes but who are now looking to begin studying scripture more closely.

To order a copy of this book, please turn to the order form on page 159.

The People's Bible Commentary

For Christians, Deuteronomy is one of the three books most quoted in the New Testament, along with Psalms and Isaiah. Studying it is a key part of seeing how the Bible fits together as a whole, and how the Old Testament lays a theological basis for Christian faith. This PBC commentary is written by Dr Philip Johnston, who is Director of Studies at Wycliffe Hall, Oxford.

DEUTERONOMY 6:1–9

FAITH IN *a* NUTSHELL

Long sermons aren't fashionable any more. Two centuries ago, many Christians regularly sat through hour-long sermons, with numerous elaborate points and sub-points. How much they actually listened is another matter! Today few of us would have the patience to listen for so long. And of those who had patience, even fewer would have the ability, since we're so used to variety in communication, the multi-media presentation or constantly changing TV image. Moses gives a long and dense sermon in the next few chapters, beginning with phrases we've already met (6:1–3), and repeatedly exhorting his hearers and listeners to faith and obedience. So it's helpful that he starts with the most basic aspect of all—what we would call the bottom line.

Shema, yisra'el

Could you sum up your faith in ten words or less? Paul's phrase 'Jesus Christ is Lord' gives the essence of Christianity… For Jews it is 'Hear, O Israel: the Lord is our God, the Lord alone' (v. 4). This is commonly called the 'Shema' (pronounced *sh'mah*, the Hebrew word for 'hear'). For several millennia pious Jews have recited it every morning and evening. Children should learn these as their first words, and the dying should repeat them as their last. This is the bottom line of Jewish faith.

Interestingly, there are different views as to what exactly the Shema means. Of the six words in Hebrew, the first two are straightforward: 'Hear, Israel'. The remaining four words are 'Yahweh, our-God,

Yahweh, one'… These four words do not include a verb, so can be fitted together differently. The phrase is sometimes translated as 'The Lord is our God, the Lord is one'—two brief statements about Yahweh. The first stresses his relationship to Israel, the second his nature. However, the second of these statements would only have been relevant after Christians started describing God as Trinity, thus affirming the different Jewish view of God. It would not have been particularly meaningful in the ancient world. Hence many people think that the original meaning of the phrase was 'Yahweh is God, Yahweh *alone*'… What God commands in the very first commandment, his people now repeat in a credal statement. They have only one God, Yahweh, to whom they give sole allegiance.

To us this may seem inconsequential. In the ancient polytheistic world, it was revolutionary. Every nation had its major gods and a host of minor ones. In the 14th century BC, the Egyptian Pharaoh Akhenaten tried to replace the plethora of Egyptian deities with the single Sun-God, worshipped in an austere non-moral religion. As soon as he died, however, his more famous son Tutankhamun… put everything back to normal. In Israel, there was a constant temptation to worship other gods, as the prophets repeatedly condemn, and as some archaeological finds now confirm. For Israel, there should only ever be one God, their God Yahweh. This was the bottom line.

Love and devotion

But faith needs action. The Shema is followed by the equally famous command to love God with heart, soul and might (v. 5), a command cited in the New Testament as the first great commandment (Matthew 22:37). Love of God demands all our devotion, all our being, all our energy. We note that here, as so often, fear (v. 2) and love (v. 5) are brought together not as opposites but as complementary aspects of the same attitude to God.

How do you love God? The following chapters spell this out for Israel, but already here we note the other verbs used: observe diligently (v. 3), keep (v. 6), recite/talk (v. 7), bind/write (vv. 8–9). It should be a constant preoccupation, inculcated in children and constantly before their eyes. Verses 8–9 are still often taken literally, with these and other key verses kept in little boxes bound to the forehead (in *tefillin*)… We may not see the need to take this command literally, but we should take it equally seriously. After all, Jesus endorsed it, and enabled us to love God by demonstrating a similar love for us.

Reflection

What would I like my last words to be?

To order a copy of this book, please turn to the order form on page 159.

For reflection:
'Search the scriptures'

Believers keep up and maintain their walk with God by reading of his holy word. 'Search the scriptures,' says our blessed Lord, 'for these are they that testify of me.' And the royal Psalmist tells us 'that God's word was a light unto his feet, and a lantern unto his paths'; and he makes it one property of a good man, 'that his delight is in the law of the Lord, and that he exercises himself therein day and night' … For whatsoever was written aforetime was written for our learning. And the word of God is profitable for reproof, for correction, and for instruction in righteousness, and every way sufficient to make every true child of God thoroughly furnished unto every good work.

If we once get above our Bibles, and cease making the written word of God our sole rule both as to faith and practice, we shall soon lie open to all manner of delusion, and be in great danger of making shipwreck of faith and a good conscience…

The scriptures are called the lively oracles of God: not only because they are generally made use of to beget in us a new life, but also to keep up and increase it in the soul. The apostle Peter, in his second epistle, prefers it even to seeing Christ transfigured upon the mount. For after he had said, chapter 1:18, 'This voice which came from heaven we heard, when we were with him in the holy mount'; he adds, 'We have also a more sure word of prophecy; whereunto ye do well that ye take heed, as unto a light shining in a dark place, until the day dawn, and the day-star arise in your hearts': that is, till we shake off these bodies, and see Jesus face to face. Till then we must see and converse with him through the glass of his word. We must make his testimonies our counsellors, and daily, with Mary, sit at Jesus' feet, by faith hearing his word. We shall then by happy experience find, that they are spirit and life, meat indeed and drink indeed, to our souls.

The scriptures are called the lively oracles of God

Secondly, believers keep up and maintain their walk with God by secret prayer. The spirit of grace is always accompanied with the spirit of supplication. It is the very breath of the new creature, the fan of the divine life, whereby the spark of holy fire, kindled in the soul by God, is not only kept in, but raised into a flame. A neglect of secret prayer has been frequently an inlet to many spiritual diseases, and has been attended with fatal consequences... It is one of the most noble parts of the believers' spiritual armour. 'Praying always,' says the apostle, 'with all manner of supplication'. 'Watch and pray,' says our Lord, 'that ye enter not into temptation.' ... Not that our Lord would have us always upon our knees, or in our closets, to the neglect of our other relative duties. But he means, that our souls should be kept in a praying frame... O prayer! Prayer! It brings and keeps God and man together. It raises man up to God, and brings God down to man. If you would there, O believers, keep up your walk with God; pray, pray without ceasing. Be much in secret, set prayer. And when you are about the common business of life... send, from time to time, short letters post to heaven upon the wings of faith. They will reach the very heart of God, and return to you again loaded with spiritual blessings.

Thirdly, holy and frequent meditation is another blessed means of keeping up a believer's walk with God. 'Prayer, reading, temptation, and meditation,' says Luther, 'make a minister.' And they also make and perfect a Christian. Meditation to the soul, is the same as digestion to the body... For meditation is a kind of silent prayer, whereby the soul is frequently as it were carried out of itself to God, and in a degree made like unto those blessed spirits, who by a kind of immediate intuition always behold the face of our heavenly Father. None but those happy souls that have been accustomed to this divine employ, can tell what a blessed promoter of the divine life, meditation is... And whilst the believer is musing on the works and word of God, especially that work of works, that wonder of wonders, that mystery of godliness, 'God manifest in the flesh', the Lamb of God slain for the sins of the world, he frequently feels the fire of divine love kindle, so that he is obliged to speak with his tongue, and tell of the loving-kindness of the Lord to his soul. Be frequent therefore in meditation, all ye that desire to keep up and maintain a close and uniform walk with the most high God.

Our souls should be kept in a praying frame

From 'Walking with God', a sermon preached by George Whitfield (1714–70).

New Daylight © BRF 2005

The Bible Reading Fellowship
First Floor, Elsfield Hall, 15–17 Elsfield Way, Oxford OX2 8FG
Tel: 01865 319700; Fax: 01865 319701
E-mail: enquiries@brf.org.uk
Website: www.brf.org.uk

ISBN 1 84101 270 X

Distributed in Australia by:
Willow Connection, PO Box 288, Brookvale, NSW 2100.
Tel: 02 9948 3957; Fax: 02 9948 8153;
E-mail: info@willowconnection.com.au
Available also from all good Christian bookshops in Australia.
For individual and group subscriptions in Australia:
Mrs Rosemary Morrall, PO Box W35, Wanniassa, ACT 2903.

Distributed in New Zealand by:
Scripture Union Wholesale, PO Box 760, Wellington
Tel: 04 385 0421; Fax: 04 384 3990; E-mail: suwholesale@clear.net.nz

Distributed in the USA by:
The Bible Reading Fellowship, PO Box 380, Winter Park,
Florida 32790-0380
Tel: 407 628 4330 or 800 749 4331; Fax: 407 647 2406;
E-mail: brf@biblereading.org; Website: www.biblereading.org

Publications distributed to more than 60 countries

BRF is a Christian charity committed to resourcing the spiritual journey of adults and children alike. For adults, BRF publishes Bible reading notes and books and offers an annual programme of quiet days and retreats. Under its children's imprint *Barnabas*, BRF publishes a wide range of books for those working with children under 11 in school, church and home. BRF's *Barnabas Ministry* team offers INSET sessions for primary teachers, training for children's leaders in church, quiet days, and a range of events to enable children themselves to engage with the Bible and its message.

We need your help if we are to make a real impact on the local church and community. In an increasingly secular world people need even more help with their Bible reading, their prayer and their discipleship. We can do something about this, but our resources are limited. With your help, if we all do a little, together we can make a huge difference.

How can you help?

- You could support BRF's ministry with a donation or standing order (using the response form overleaf).

- You could consider making a bequest to BRF in your will, and so give lasting support to our work. (We have a leaflet available with more information about this, which can be requested using the form overleaf.)

- And, most important of all, you could support BRF with your prayers.

Whatever you can do or give, we thank you for your support.

BRF – resourcing your spiritual journey

BRF MINISTRY APPEAL RESPONSE FORM

Name _____

Address _____

_____ Postcode _____

Telephone _____ Email _____

(tick as appropriate)

Gift Aid Declaration

❏ I am a UK taxpayer. I want BRF to treat as Gift Aid Donations all donations I make from 6 April 2000 until I notify you otherwise.

Signature _____ Date _____

❏ I would like to support BRF's ministry with a regular donation by standing order (please complete the Banker's Order below).

Standing Order – Banker's Order

To the Manager, Name of Bank/Building Society _____

Address _____

_____ Postcode _____

Sort Code _____ Account Name _____

Account No _____

Please pay Royal Bank of Scotland plc, London Drummonds Branch, 49 Charing Cross, London SW1A 2DX (Sort Code 16-00-38), for the account of BRF A/C No. 00774151

The sum of _____ pounds on ___ /____ /____ (insert date your standing order starts) and thereafter the same amount on the same day of each month until further notice.

Signature _____ Date _____

Single donation

❏ I enclose my cheque/credit card/Switch card details for a donation of £5 £10 £25 £50 £100 £250 (other) £ _____ to support BRF's ministry

Credit/ Switch card no. ▢▢▢▢▢▢▢▢▢▢▢▢▢▢▢▢▢▢▢▢

Expires ▢▢ ▢▢   Issue no. of Switch card ▢▢▢

Signature _____ Date _____

(Where appropriate, on receipt of your donation, we will send you a Gift Aid form)

❏ Please send me information about making a bequest to BRF in my will.

Please detach and send this completed form to: Richard Fisher, BRF, First Floor, Elsfield Hall, 15–17 Elsfield Way, Oxford OX2 8FG. BRF is a Registered Charity (No.233280)

ND0305

BIBLE READING RESOURCES PACK

A pack of resources and ideas to help to promote Bible reading in your church is available from BRF. The pack, which will be of use at any time during the year, includes sample editions of the notes, magazine articles, leaflets about BRF Bible reading resources and much more. Unless you specify the month in which you would like the pack sent, we will send it immediately on receipt of your order. We greatly appreciate your donations towards the cost of producing the pack (without them we would not be able to make the pack available) and we welcome your comments about the contents of the pack and your ideas for future ones.

This coupon should be sent to:

BRF
First Floor
Elsfield Hall
15–17 Elsfield Way
Oxford
OX2 8FG

Name ———————————————————————

Address ———————————————————————

———————————————————————————

——————————————————— Postcode ————————

Telephone ————————————————————

Email ———————————————————————————

Please send me ———— Bible Reading Resources Pack(s)

Please send the pack now/ in ———————————(month).

I enclose a donation for £ ———— towards the cost of the pack.

BRF is a Registered Charity

NEW DAYLIGHT SUBSCRIPTIONS

❏ I would like to give a gift subscription (please complete both name and address sections below)

❏ I would like to take out a subscription myself (complete name and address details only once)

This completed coupon should be sent with appropriate payment to BRF. Alternatively, please write to us quoting your name, address, the subscription you would like for either yourself or a friend (with their name and address), the start date and credit card number, expiry date and signature if paying by credit card.

Gift subscription name _____

Gift subscription address _____

_____

_____Postcode _____

Please send beginning with the January / May / September 2006 issue: (delete as applicable)

(please tick box)	UK	SURFACE	AIR MAIL
NEW DAYLIGHT	❏ £11.70	❏ £13.05	❏ £15.30
NEW DAYLIGHT 3-year sub	❏ £29.25		
NEW DAYLIGHT LARGE PRINT	❏ £16.80	❏ £20.40	❏ £24.90

Please complete the payment details below and send your coupon, with appropriate payment to: **BRF, First Floor, Elsfield Hall, 15–17 Elsfield Way, Oxford OX2 8FG.**

Your name _____

Your address _____

_____

_____Postcode _____

Total enclosed £ _____ (cheques should be made payable to 'BRF')

Payment by cheque ❏ postal order ❏ Visa ❏ Mastercard ❏ Switch ❏

Card number: ⬚⬚⬚⬚⬚⬚⬚⬚⬚⬚⬚⬚⬚⬚⬚⬚⬚⬚

Expiry date of card: ⬚⬚⬚⬚   Issue number (Switch): ⬚⬚⬚⬚

Signature (essential if paying by credit/Switch card) _____

❏ Please do not send me further information about BRF publications.

BRF resources are available from your local Christian bookshop. BRF is a Registered Charity

ND0305

BRF PUBLICATIONS ORDER FORM

Please ensure that you complete and send off both sides of this order form.

Please send me the following book(s):	Quantity	Price	Total
390 0 O Come, Emmanuel (G. Giles)	_____	£7.99	_____
425 7 Women of the Word (ed. J. Stead)	_____	£6.99	_____
360 9 Walking with Jesus thru Advent and Christmas (M. McBride)	_____	£9.99	_____
424 9 The Story of Christmas (S. Jeffs & J. Haysom)	_____	£5.99	_____
192 4 PBC: Leviticus and Numbers (M. Butterworth)	_____	£7.99	_____
318 8 PBC: Deuteronomy (P. Johnston)	_____	£8.99	_____
095 2 PBC: Joshua and Judges (S. Mathewson)	_____	£7.99	_____
242 4 PBC: Ruth, Esther, Ecclesiastes, Song, Lamentations (R. Fyall)	_____	£8.99	_____
030 8 PBC: 1 & 2 Samuel (H. Mowvley)	_____	£7.99	_____
118 5 PBC: 1 & 2 Kings (S. Dawes)	_____	£7.99	_____
070 7 PBC: Chronicles—Nehemiah (M. Tunnicliffe)	_____	£7.99	_____
094 4 PBC: Job (K. Dell)	_____	£7.99	_____
031 6 PBC: Psalms 1—72 (D. Coggan)	_____	£8.99	_____
065 0 PBC: Psalms 73—150 (D. Coggan)	_____	£7.99	_____
071 5 PBC: Proverbs (E. Mellor)	_____	£7.99	_____
087 1 PBC: Jeremiah (R. Mason)	_____	£7.99	_____
040 5 PBC: Ezekiel (E. Lucas)	_____	£7.99	_____
245 9 PBC: Hosea—Micah (P. Gooder)	_____	£8.99	_____
028 6 PBC: Nahum—Malachi (G. Emmerson)	_____	£7.99	_____
191 6 PBC: Matthew (J. Proctor)	_____	£7.99	_____
046 4 PBC: Mark (D. France)	_____	£8.99	_____
027 8 PBC: Luke (H. Wansbrough)	_____	£7.99	_____
029 4 PBC: John (R.A. Burridge)	_____	£7.99	_____
082 0 PBC: Romans (J. Dunn)	_____	£7.99	_____
122 3 PBC: 1 Corinthians (J. Murphy-O'Connor)	_____	£7.99	_____
073 1 PBC: 2 Corinthians (A. Besançon Spencer)	_____	£7.99	_____
012 X PBC: Galatians and 1 & 2 Thessalonians (J. Fenton)	_____	£7.99	_____
047 2 PBC: Ephesians—Colossians & Philemon (M. Maxwell)	_____	£7.99	_____
119 3 PBC: Timothy, Titus and Hebrews (D. France)	_____	£7.99	_____
092 8 PBC: James—Jude (F. Moloney)	_____	£7.99	_____
363 3 PBC: Revelation (M. Maxwell)	_____	£8.99	_____

Total cost of books £ _____

Postage and packing (see over) £ _____

TOTAL £ _____

See over for payment details. All prices are correct at time of going to press, are subject to the prevailing rate of VAT and may be subject to change without prior warning.

BRF resources are available from your local Christian bookshop. BRF is a Registered Charity

PAYMENT DETAILS

Please complete the payment details below and send with appropriate payment and completed order form to:

**BRF, First Floor, Elsfield Hall,
15–17 Elsfield Way, Oxford OX2 8FG**

Name _____

Address _____

_____

_____ Postcode _____

Telephone _____

Email _____

Total enclosed £ _____(cheques should be made payable to 'BRF')

Payment by cheque ❏ postal order ❏ Visa ❏ Mastercard ❏ Switch ❏

Card number: ☐☐☐☐☐☐☐☐☐☐☐☐☐☐☐☐☐☐☐☐

Expiry date of card: ☐☐☐☐   Issue number (Switch): ☐☐☐☐

Signature (essential if paying by credit/Switch card) _____

ALTERNATIVE WAYS TO ORDER

Christian bookshops: All good Christian bookshops stock BRF publications. For your nearest stockist, please contact BRF.

POSTAGE AND PACKING CHARGES				
order value	UK	Europe	Surface	Air Mail
£7.00 & under	£1.25	£3.00	£3.50	£5.50
£7.01–£30.00	£2.25	£5.50	£6.50	£10.00
Over £30.00	free	prices on request		

Telephone: The BRF office is open between 09.15 and 17.30. To place your order, phone 01865 319700; fax 01865 319701.

Web: Visit www.brf.org.uk

Please do not send me further information about BRF publications.

BRF is a Registered Charity